FOR KING & EMPIRE

THE CANADIANS AT MOUNT SORREL

June 2nd-14th, 1916

A Social History and Battlefield Tour

by N. M. Christie

FOR KING & EMPIRE; VOLUME VIII

CEF BOOKS
2000

Canadian Cataloguing in Publication Data
Christie, N.M.
     The Canadians at Mount Sorrel, June 1916
(For King & Empire: v. 8)
ISBN 1-896979-14-9
     1. Sorrel, Mount (Belgium), Battle of, 1916. 2. Canada. Canadian Army—History—World War, 1914-1918. 3. World War, 1914-1918, Battlefields—Belgium—Sorrel, Mount—Tours. I. Title. II. Series: Christie, N.M. For King & Empire; v.8.

D542.M8C48   1999 940.4'272   C99-900695-9

Published by: CEF BOOKS
                   P.O. Box 40083
                   Ottawa, Ontario, K1V 0W8
                   1-613-823-7000

 Publication of this book has been
supported by the Canadian War Museum.

Other books in this series

Front cover: Ypres Reservoir Cemetery, Ypres, Belgium.

Acknowledgements: The Author would like to thank Mr. Gary Roncetti of Port Perry, Sheila Hanratty of Ottawa, and Dave and Linda Horton of Manotick, Ontario.

The flies! Oh God the flies
That soiled the sacred dead.
To see them swarm from dead men's eyes
And share the soldier's bread!
Nor think I now forget
The filth and stench of war,
The corpses on the parapet,
The maggots on the floor.

A.P. Herbert

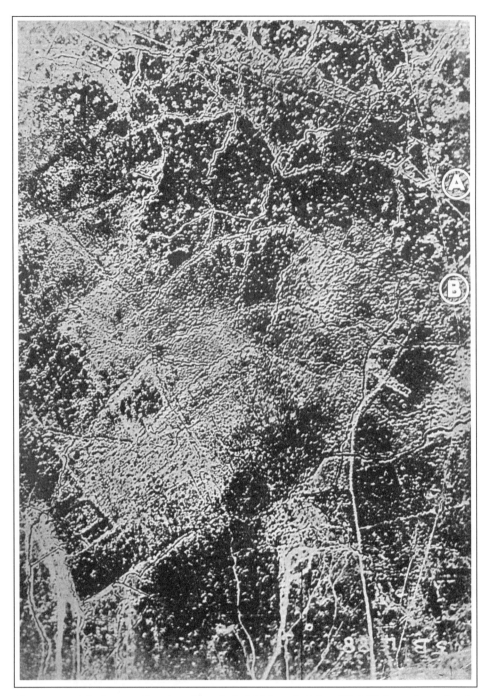

German aerial photograph taken June 3rd, 1916, at height of 7,500 feet, of trenches in Sanctuary Wood, showing the results of the bombardment of June 2nd. At "A" are the German front line trenches, and at "B" are the British front line trenches. This photograph was found among the effects of a captured German Officer.

Table of Contents

Corporal Lewis George Eastman, DCM, 3rd (Toronto Regiment)Battalion. Killed in action at Mount Sorrel, June 13th, 1916. His remains were found in 1922, and buried in Bedford House Cemetery.

Introduction to the Battle of Mount Sorrel, June 1916

The Battle of Mount Sorrel was in many ways the true face of the First World War. It had horror, slaughter, mass destruction and the futility of having no effect on the outcome of the war. In addition the fact that it has been completely forgotten only lends to it being the "perfect" representation of a First World War battle. Unfortunately it was not unique. During the Great War there were hundreds of ugly, little battles or actions as they were often called. They had no strategic significance and were played out, almost like a game. It was one commander trying to outwit his opponent to secure a slightly better observation or to impress his superiors.

The Battle of Mount Sorrel was precisely that. A German General (Würtemburger) wanted to improve his position on the heights south-east of Ypres. To do so he unleashed a devastating explosive force of artillery and underground mines on a one km front between two high points, Hill 62 and Mount Sorrel. His unlucky opponent was the newly arrived and inexperienced 3rd Canadian Division.

For Canada the Battle of Mount Sorrel was a turning point. It marked the beginning of a progression that would ultimately result in the undisciplined colonials becoming the most formidable attacking Corps on the Western Front. The Battle would challenge the three infantry divisions of the newly-formed Canadian Corps. It would test their fighting strength, tenacity and resilience against a determined enemy. In the end the Canadians hung on at a heavy cost of almost 10,000 killed, wounded or taken prisoner. They lost two Generals and six Colonels. The 3rd Division had been shattered, and Canadian confidence severely shaken. Mount Sorrel was definitely a bloody nose for Canadian arms, but they had regained the lost trenches; they had come back.

The Battle of Mount Sorrel was only an episode in the far greater and more infamous story of the "Ypres Salient", 1914-1918 (even the Battle of Passchendaele is only a chapter).

The "Salient" was the front line for four years of war, the

scene of three major battles, and the venue of the first use of poisonous gas and the flame-thrower. "Ypres" became the grave of 500,000 men and the stench of rotting corpses pervaded the memories of all who served there. It was "Hell on Earth", or as Seigfreid Sasson wrote, "Here was the world's worst wound."

Today Ypres goes by its Flemish name, IEPER. But the modern prosperity cannot disguise the gaping wound that was the "Ypres Salient." The thousands of graves in the hundreds of cemeteries that surround the region belie any idea that the past is gone. There is no place on earth that any tourist can so easily touch another era. It is still the host to the ghosts, the sounds and the smells of times gone-by. Standing in the Grote Markt it doesn't take long for the sounds of traffic to be transformed into the sounds of boots tramping on the cobblestones. Here was war at its most barren: pure killing and destroying. It is the presence of these pure destructive energies transcending the aura of modern Ieper, that makes this connection to another time so imperial. So regardless of the date or of other facades this place will always be YPRES!

In those days all soldiers knew the odds of life and death of being in "the Salient". In song they voiced their fears.

"Far far from Ypres I long to be,
Where the Allemands cannot get me;
Thinking of me crouching where the worms creep,
Waiting for the Sergeant to sing me asleep.
Sleep? Sergeant - sleep?
Does anyone sleep?
They certainly sleep; everyone sleeps,
But not - surely not, Sergeant!
Not in the Yeep-pres Salient.

When taking this passage to this other time remember the Dead; the fallen "who feed the guns," for amongst them were 16,000 Canadians.

Components of the Canadian Corps
The Battle of Mount Sorrel, June 1916

1ST CANADIAN DIVISION

1ST INFANTRY BRIGADE	2ND INFANTRY BRIGADE	3RD INFANTRY BRIGADE
1ST BATTALION (WESTERN ONTARIO)	5TH BATTALION (SASKATCHEWAN)	13TH BATTALION (BLACK WATCH OF MONTREAL)
2ND BATTALION (EASTERN ONTARIO)	7TH BATTALION (BRITISH COLUMBIA)	14TH BATTALION (ROYAL MONTREAL REGIMENT)
3RD BATTALION (TORONTO REGIMENT)	8TH BATTALION (90TH RIFLES OF WINNIPEG)	15TH BATTALION (48TH HIGHLANDERS OF TORONTO)
4TH BATTALION (CENTRAL ONTARIO)	10TH BATTALION (ALBERTA)	16TH BATTALION (CANADIAN SCOTTISH)

2ND CANADIAN DIVISION

4TH INFANTRY BRIGADE	5TH INFANTRY BRIGADE	6TH INFANTRY BRIGADE
18TH BATTALION (WESTERN ONTARIO)	22ND BATTALION (CANADIEN-FRANÇAIS)	27TH BATTALION (CITY OF WINNIPEG)
19TH BATTALION (CENTRAL ONTARIO)	24TH BATTALION (VICTORIA RIFLES OF MONTREAL)	28TH BATTALION (SASKATCHEWAN)
20TH BATTALION (CENTRAL ONTARIO)	25TH BATTALION (NOVA SCOTIA)	29TH BATTALION (BRITISH COLUMBIA)
21ST BATTALION (EASTERN ONTARIO)	26TH BATTALION (NEW BRUNSWICK)	31ST BATTALION (ALBERTA)

3RD CANADIAN DIVISION

7TH INFANTRY BRIGADE	8TH INFANTRY BRIGADE	9TH INFANTRY BRIGADE
ROYAL CANADIAN REGIMENT	1ST CANADIAN MOUNTED RIFLES (SASKATCHEWAN)	43RD BATTALION (CAMERON HIGHLANDERS OF WINNIPEG)
PRINCESS PATRICIA'S CANADIAN LIGHT INFANTRY	2ND CANADIAN MOUNTED RIFLES (BRITISH COLUMBIA)	52ND BATTALION (NEW ONTARIO)
42ND BATTALION (BLACK WATCH OF MONTREAL)	4TH CANADIAN MOUNTED RIFLES (CENTRAL ONTARIO)	58TH BATTALION (CENTRAL ONTARIO)
49TH BATTALION (ALBERTA)	5TH CANADIAN MOUNTED RIFLES (QUEBEC)	60TH BATTALION (VICTORIA RIFLES OF MONTREAL)

The Lille Gate, Ypres. April-May 1919

(PUBLIC ARCHIVES OF CANADA PA 4617)

Getting There

Ypres or Ieper (as it is now called) is located in western Belgium, 20 km north of the Belgian/French border. It is easily accessible from Paris (300 km) and Brussels (100 km). From London, it is a two-hour drive to Dover, a 75 minute ferry ride to Calais, and a 45 minute drive from Calais. The opening of the Channel Tunnel has made a direct rail link from London to Lille, France, which is close to the Belgian border. Check with the Tourist Board for details. Rental cars are available in any of the above-mentioned cities and tourist offices can supply routes and details of hotels.

In Flanders the main language is Flemish, a form of Dutch. Belgians in general speak several languages and English is widely understood.

There are approximately 24 Belgian francs (2000) to one Canadian dollar. In Ypres, French francs are also accepted in most stores and restaurants. Credit cards, such as VISA, Access or MasterCard are accepted, but please check with the hotel where you are staying. Always visit the Tourism Office to obtain information on accommodation or events of interest.

What To Bring

Weather is very changeable in this part of Europe. Days can start sunny and change quickly to rain, hail or even a sprinkling of snow. Above all, be prepared for wet weather. For example, the average temperature in Belgium in July varies from 12 to 24°C.

Other than the obvious, a passport, traveller's checks and appropriate clothing, bring the following to ensure a successful trip:

- a bottle opener and cork screw
- binoculars
- a camera (with 100 and 200 ASA film)
- a compass
- rubber boots
- National Geographic Institute maps 1:25,000, numbers 28/1-2, 28/3-4 and 28/5-6 (these can be obtained at the Tourist Office in Ypres)
- Michelin map No. 51 (preferably the Commonwealth War Graves Commission overprint, showing all the cemeteries)
- reference books (do your research before departure)
- a journal to record the details of your visit, because you will forget.

About Ypres / Ieper

Ypres (Ieper, Ypern) lies in the quiet, farmland of Flanders in western Belgium. For centuries this now-modern town has been one of Europe's strategic battlegrounds. In the Middle Ages, the town was one of Belgium's jewels, the strength and wealth of Flanders. It was the centre of culture and commerce, with a flourishing textile trade. Ypres was in its greatest glory in the 13th century and had a population of 40,000 people, with another 150,000 in the surrounding region.

It was at this time construction of the town's most famous building, the great Lakenhalle (Cloth Hall), a monument to Ypres's textile industry, was begun. Taking 100 years to build, this impressive covered market allowed ships to moor alongside to load and discharge cargoes onto a covered quay along the banks of the Yperlee. The Nieuwerck (Town Hall), now a tourist office, was completed some 300 years later. The upper storey, once used for storage, today houses a museum and a concert hall. From its 70-metre belfry, the hours are sounded by a 49-bell carillon.

Ypres

Ypres' flourishing trade dropped significantly in 1383, when the town was attacked by troops from England and Ghent. Although Ypres resisted the siege, many weavers left, taking the livelihood of the town with them. By the 1500s, the population of the town was 5,000 and its importance had diminished.

Over the last 600 years, Ypres has been attacked by the Spaniards, the French, the Austrians and the Dutch. When Ypres became French in 1678, the city's defence works were revamped by renowned French military engineer Marshal Vauban. These defences were able to withstand the wars of 1689-1712, but the end of the 18th century witnessed the dismantling of many of the town's defences. After Waterloo, when Belgium united with the Netherlands, Ypres again strongly fortified against any possible French invasion. In the 1830s Ypres became a part of the newly independent country of Belgium and soon afterwards the Belgian government decided Ypres no longer needed to be fortified. Walls and ramparts were removed to make room for railways and old gates were demolished to allow wider passage on the roads. Today the only gate left is the Lille Gate or Rijselsepoort on the southern side of town.

In 1914 Ypres once again lay in the path of warring nations. The German cavalry rode into the town on October 13th. The next day the British Expeditionary Force drove them out and retook Ypres. Later in October the First Battle of Ypres was fought. During the fighting a great artillery barrage, which began on November 22nd, damaged the ancient buildings and set the Cloth Hall on fire. Civilians suffered considerably but were not evacuated until the Second Battle of Ypres in 1915. It was in April/May 1915 that the Cloth Hall, the Church of St. Martin and other important buildings were destroyed. Although many civilians returned to the ruins of their homes during the comparatively quiet times in 1916, Ypres was essentially under military control until the Third Battle of Ypres, July -November 1917. In the spring of 1918 Ypres was nearly lost in the great German Offensive, but French and British troops held on. It was not until the final Allied Offensive, September 28th, 1918, which included Belgian, French and British soldiers, that the town was finally beyond German observation and artillery fire. Damage from the war was so catastrophic that the entire town had to be rebuilt from scratch. Ypres was rebuilt, brick-by-brick, after the First World War.

In the Second World War Belgium was once again a trampling ground for invading German Armies. There was some fighting between the advancing Germans and rear-guard forces of the British Army in 1940. From May 1940 until 1944 Ypres was under the heel of the occupying Germans. In September 1944 Ypres was liberated by the 1st Polish Armoured Division.

The prominent architecture in Ypres today is its refashioned St. Martin's Cathedral, the towering Cloth Hall and reconstructed 17th century façades in much of the town. The Grote Markt (Great Market) is the town centre and is surrounded by the Courthouse, the old Town Hall, the Kasselrijgebouw (with seven deadly sins carved on its façade) and numerous cafés and restaurants where you can enjoy a beer, a coffee or a good lunch. Market day is Saturday morning.

The tourist office is in the Cloth Hall (tel. 57 200724) and offers comprehensive tourist information in English, as well as guidebooks, maps and leaflets listing hotels and restaurants.

Hotels: *Hotel Ariane*, Slachthuisstraat 58 (near Grote Markt), 8900 Ieper, tel. 57 218218; *Hotel Rabbit*, Industrielaan 19, 8900 Ieper, tel. 57 217000; *Regina Hotel*, Grote Markt 45, 8900 Ieper, tel. 57 218888, Kasteelhof 't Hooghe, Meenseweg 481, 8902 Ieper, tel. 57 468787; *Hotel Sultan*, Grote Markt 33, 8900 Ieper, tel. 57 219030, The Shell Hole Hotel, D'hondstraaat, 54, 8900 Ieper, tel. 57-208758.

Ypres, The Menin Gate, April-May 1919

(PUBLIC ARCHIVES OF CANADA PA 4618)

There are many restaurants in and around Ypres that cater to a wide variety of tastes and pocketbooks. Check with the Tourist Office for particulars.

There are a number of interesting museums pertaining to the First World War in the Ypres area. *In Flanders Fields, Interactive Museum World War I*, Cloth Hall, Grote Markt, 8900 Ieper, tel. 57 200724; *Hooge Crater 14-18 Museum*, Meenseweg 467, 8902 Zillebeke, tel. 57 468446; *Hill 60-Queen Victoria Rifles Museum*, Zwarteleenstraat 40, 8902 Zillebeke, tel. 57 206276; *Hill 62-Sanctuary Wood Museum*, Canadalaan 26, 8902 Zillebeke, tel. 57 466373.

This guide uses place names of the 1914-1918 period. Below is a list of place names as you will see them today (on the left) and as they were known during the war (on the right).

Modern	**1914-1918**
Boezinge	Boesinghe
Dikkebus	Dickebusch
t'Hoge	Hooge
Ieper	Ypres
Langemark	Langemarck
Menen	Menin
Passendale	Passchendaele
Poelkapelle	Poelcapelle
Poperinge	Poperinghe
Reningelst	Reninghelst
St.Elooi	St.Eloi
Vlamertinge	Vlamertinghe
Voormezele	Voormezeele
Zillebeke	Zillebeke

The Front Line in May 1916

THE BATTLE OF MOUNT SORREL, JUNE 2ND TO 13TH, 1916

HISTORICAL OVERVIEW

1916 was to be the year of victory. Plans for great, decisive offensives were afoot. But in the end it became a year of blood and stalemate, a year in which more than two million men would be killed or wounded in the battles of Verdun and the Somme alone. The great optimism of the new year was quickly dashed by the major German offensive at Verdun in February 1916 and further dimmed when the invincible Royal Navy lost 14 ships, including three battle-cruisers and more than 6,000 souls in the Battle of Jutland. To make matters worse April 1916 witnessed the surrender of the besieged 6th British Division to Turkish forces at Kut-el-Amara in Mesopotamia (Iraq).

However the British still optimistically believed that the forthcoming Battle of the Somme would be a smashing success; the decisive blow to end the war. Consequently all eyes, all resources, and all material were being sent to the British Army build-up for the upcoming Battle of the Somme, 130 km south of the Ypres Salient.

After the Second Battle of Ypres,* in May 1915, Ypres had been relegated to a secondary front. All the British Offensives in 1915 had taken place in the lowlands south of Armentieres: at Neuve Chapelle, Festubert, Aubers Ridge, Givenchy and Loos. Ypres had remained a deadly place but was not foremost in the High Commands' plans. In fact the front lines had changed little since the Second Battle of Ypres officially ended on May 24th, 1915. The Salient had been reduced to only three km deep. It ran from the Ypres Canal, four km north of Ypres, in a south-easterly direction for seven km, where it crossed the Ypres-Menin road at the small hamlet of Hooge. It continued in its south-easterly direction to Sanctuary Wood, turned south, then south-west following the eastern edge of the wood, and then ran two km along a series of high points;   Hill 62 (Tor Top),

* see For King & Empire, Volume I; The Canadians at Ypres, April 1915. CEF Books, 1999.

Observatory Ridge, Mount Sorrel, and Hill 60. It continued south-west over the Ypres-Comines railway cutting, then 1.4 km south-west, until it crossed the Ypres-Comines Canal and turned west for 1.6 km to the hamlet of St.Eloi, five km due south of Ypres. The perimeter of the Salient was roughly 16 km from Boesinghe to St.Eloi.

To say that Ypres was a secondary front was not to say it was not active. It was the deadliest, most infamous place on earth. Even in "quiet" times. "Ypres" was an on-going battle that raged along the perimeter of the Salient, both above ground and below. Poison gas, flame-throwers, massive underground explosions, bullets and constant artillery fire were the weapons used to tear both men and land apart.

It was at Ypres in April 1915 that the Germans introduced suffocating chlorine gas into the lexicon of military matters. In December 1915 they tried again to break "the Salient" by releasing phosgene gas on British troops holding the northern sector. At Hooge July 30th, 1915 the Germans introduced the flamenwerfer or flame-thrower to the world. But the most hideous warfare, was the battle launched below the ground by the miners.

In 1915 and 1916 mining warfare was a favourite of both sides. All along the Western Front the Allies and Germans fought a treacherous campaign to annihilate the enemy's miners and blow his front lines to smithereens. At Ypres the low water table did not help the miners but nor did it deter them. Under Hill 60 the fighting was particularly severe. On many occasions huge mines were exploded under the British lines and vicious battles for possession of the crater would take place. The intensity of combat was such that four Victoria Crosses were awarded for bravery at Hill 60. Similarly at Hooge mining warfare had turned the beautiful Chateau grounds to "Hell on Earth". Between July and November 1915 the grounds had been lost and regained innumerable times at considerable cost. Holding both Hill 60 and Hooge was a point of honour and woe be it to the regiment that failed in its duties. It was into these positions in the southern salient, from Hooge to St. Eloi that the Canadians came in late March 1916. They could not have been assured by what they found.

A mine goes up.

The Canadians to Spring 1916

In the Second Battle of Ypres in April 1915 the Canadian Expeditionary Force had consisted of one infantry division. Its performance against the gas and the attacking Germans had brought it praise from all corners. But one in three were killed, wounded or taken prisoner. After the battle the 1st Canadian Division was withdrawn, reinforced and shipped south to fight alongside British Divisions in the Battles of Festubert (May 1915) and Givenchy (June 1915).**

These minor battles cost the lives of 1,040 Canadians. Another 2,269 were wounded. In two months the infantry establishment of 11,000 men had suffered 9,413 casualties. A casualty rate of 86%! After Givenchy the 1st Division was moved to the Ploegsteert Wood sector, 13 km south of Ypres. They remained there in relative safety until the spring of 1916.

In the meantime recruiting in Canada had produced a Second Contingent of 30,000 men. They had arrived in England in the summer of 1915 and proceeded to Belgium in September 1915. After rudimentary training and some exposure to trench life the "2nd Canadian Division" took over the Kemmel sector, just north of the Ploegsteert Wood, and 10 km south of Ypres.

The arrival a second Division allowed for the formation of a Canadian Corps under the Command of Lieutenant-General Edwin Alderson, an English General who had commanded the 1st Canadian Division since September 1914. At the time the formation of an Army Corps based on Nationality seemed almost an afterthought. As the war progressed it would become one of the most important decisions in the development of the most efficient fighting formation on the Western Front.

The 2nd Division led a cautious life on the Kemmel front from September 1915 to March 1916. At the end of March 1916 the 2nd Division was involved in one of the most confusing and least successful battles fought by a Canadian Division in the entire war. The "Actions of St.Eloi Craters"** were fought March 27th, 1916 to April 16th, 1916. It involved fighting over a series of recently blown mine craters in front of the hamlet of St.Eloi. After two weeks of confused fighting the 2nd Division had lost

** see the upcoming Volume IX in the For King & Empire series; Other Canadian Battlefields of the Great War.

all the craters and suffered 1,373 killed, wounded and taken prisoner. Their first action of the war was a catastophic failure. The 2nd Division remained in the lines near St.Eloi until June 1916.

A third Canadian Division joined the Canadian Corps in December 1915. The appropriately named "3rd Canadian Division" consisted of the 7th, 8th and 9th infantry brigades.

The 7th Brigade was made up of: the experienced Princess Patricia's Canadian Light Infantry, who had been fighting with a British Division since December 1914; the Royal Canadian Regiment, Canada's only permanent infantry regiment, who had recently arrived from garrison duty in Bermuda; the 42nd (Black Watch of Montreal) and the 49th (Alberta) Battalions who had been in France since the fall of 1915, but had seen little action.

The 8th Brigade was composed of dismounted cavalry. Six regiments of Canadian Mounted Rifles had arrived in France and served as Corps Cavalry since the fall of 1915. Now their horses were taken away and the men of the 3rd and 6th CMR transferred to the 1st (Saskatchewan) CMR, 2nd (British Columbia) CMR, 4th (Central Ontario) CMR, and 5th (Quebec) CMR infantry battalions. They were known as the Mounted Rifles Brigade.

The 9th Brigade was formed in February-March 1916 of inexperienced battalions fresh from England. The 43rd (Cameron Highlanders of Winnipeg), 52nd (New Ontario from Port Arthur), 58th (Central Ontario) and the 60th (Victoria Rifles of Montreal) Battalions made up the 9th Brigade.

Command of the 3rd Division was given to Major-General Malcolm Mercer, a regular officer of Canada's Permanent Army. Mercer had fought in the Boer War and commanded the 1st Brigade in the Second Battle of Ypres. He was highly thought of and some felt he was the best General Canada had to offer.

At the end of March 1916 Mercer got his marching orders. His inexperienced troops were given the worst news possible. They were to hold the line from Hooge to Mount Sorrel, the most lethal sector in the Salient.

At the beginning of April 1916, while the 3rd Division had their first tours in the Salient, the 1st Division also shifted north and were assigned the always deadly Hill 60 sector. Hill 60 had been lost in February 1916 and now the men of the 1st Division were overlooked by the evil eyes of the Huns. With every stand-to the men held their breath anticipating the rumble of the ground and the sheer terror that accompanied an underground mine detonation.

To the Germans the importance of the lines held by the Canadians were the heights: Hill 62, Observatory Ridge and Mount Sorrel. In the entire Salient, it was only at these places the Germans did not occupy the heights, so it was in their interests to capture them.

Back at Headquarters, General Alderson now commanded an Army Corps of three Canadian Divisions, a fine feather in his cap at the end of his 40 year military career. But the politics of Canada's Military organization, headed by the unusual Minister of Militia, Sam Hughes, was about to turn Alderson's world upside down. Hughes was as political an animal as they come and Alderson's inexperience in having to deal with such people was his undoing. Edwin Alderson had the audacity of to be honest and to look out for the needs of his men. Amongst those needs was the withdrawal of the unreliable, Canadian-made Ross rifle used by the Canadians since 1914. The rifle jammed in rapid fire, and although an excellent target rifle, required exacting ammunition tolerances, an impossible requirement in war. By coming out against the Ross Rifle Alderson was also coming out against Hughes. The Ross was Sam Hughes' pet project and Hughes could accept no criticism of what he knew was right, even if he was wrong. Crossing Sir Sam was a dangerous venture and in no time the vindictive Minister responded by letter, indicating just how wrong General Alderson's conclusions on the Ross were. For further effect and to completely undermine Alderson's command, he copied the letter to 284 of his subordinates - all the senior officers in the Canadian Expeditionary Force!

Hughes, having no further use for the troublesome Alderson, and needing a scapegoat for the St. Eloi fiasco, pushed and got Alderson's prompt dismissal. His replacement was a British Cavalry Officer, Julian Byng. Byng was a non-conformist, who had recently been bypassed for promotion to Army commander (given to another cavalry general, junior in service). Byng accepted his lateral move as Lieutenant-General commanding the Canadian Corps on May 29th, 1916. His appointment would be the second major event that would result in the great progress of the Canadian Corps. Julian Byng would be a God-send to the Canadians. They did not know how lucky they were. Byng had little time to bask in the glory of his new position as intelligence had reported German activity opposite Mount Sorrel. The new commander thought of checking the situation out in person but pressing matters changed his mind. He ordered General Mercer to go and investigate. (See "Sir Julian Byng", page 90.)

The Defences

At the beginning of June 1916 the Canadian Corps held the southern belly of the Ypres Salient, from just north of Hooge to St.Eloi.

The 3rd Division held the left or northern flank. The Royal Canadian Regiment held the left of the line from a point 500 metres north of Hooge to just south of the Ypres-Menin road. The Hooge sector was the most vulnerable to German fire and its defences "consisted of eight outposts inaccessible by daylight, the intervening space being both open to view and waist deep in water and slime." The frontage south of the road "consisted of a wet trench whose parapet had been badly knocked about, with a long dilapidated and exposed communication trench leading to it." The RCR's regimental history continues, "Between the lines were the remains of French and German soldiers killed months before, while it was a common occurrence to turn up bodies when endeavouring to repair the trenches ... Sniping, machine gun fire and shelling were constant, enfilading the whole position. The thankfulness which all experienced at the end of a tour in this Sector was equalled only by the gloom of the relieving troops." The front line of the sector was backed-up by a support trench which ran 500 metres behind the front line trench.

The line then jumped 350 metres through an unoccupied area know as "the Gap". The next sector was know as the Sanctuary Wood sector and at the beginning of June its 900

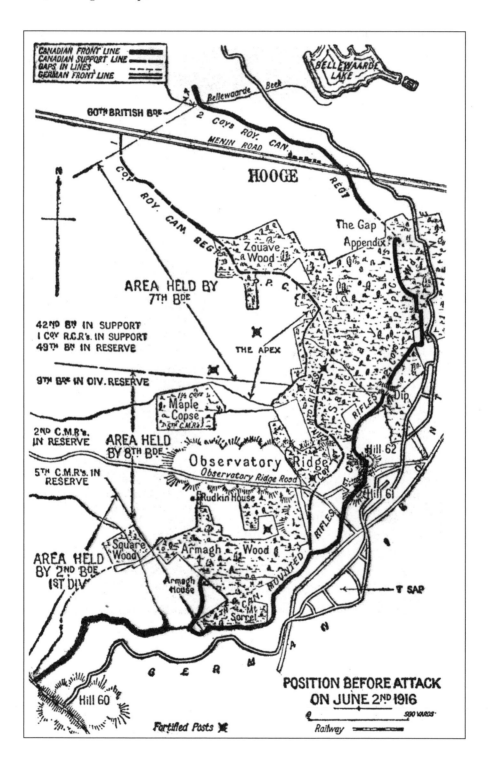

POSITION BEFORE ATTACK
ON JUNE 2ND 1916

metres were held by the PPCLI. It was the apex of the Salient in June 1916 and was defended by two strong points (SP) at "the Appendix" , between "the Gap" on the north, and "the Loop", 400 metres south.

Both the front lines ran very close together here, but the Germans had by far the most commanding position. From the "Birdcage", a German strong point built on the grounds of Stirling Castle, the Canadians could easily be enfiladed. The overall defence depended on the strength of the support line 400 metres behind the front. Both trench systems were held in strength with supports close at hand and more reserves waiting in Ypres. An added defensive feature was the complex of trenches and strong points than ran through Sanctuary Wood.

The honour of holding the heights, Hills 61/ 62 (also known as Tor Top) and Mount Sorrel, fell to two of the recently dismounted cavalry regiments, the 1st CMR (Saskatchewan) and 4th CMR (Central Ontario) Battalions, respectively. The defences along the 1.4 km front, through the wooded hills, were similar to that of Sanctuary Wood: defence in depth via a complex of support trenches and strong points.

As part of the reinforcing plan the 42nd (Black Watch of Montreal) and 5th CMR Battalions were held less than two km behind the front for rapid deployment if required.

To the right of the 3rd Division two battalions of the 1st Division held the infamous Hill 60 sector. The 5th (Saskatchewan) and the 8th (90th Rifles of Winnipeg) Battalions held the 900 metre front. The 7th (British Columbia) Battalion closely supported them.

The 2nd Division defended the right of the Canadian line. The 20th (Central Ontario) held from the railway cutting to a deadly position know as "the Bluff". "The Bluff", like Hill 60 and Hooge, had an ominous reputation for sudden death. Its trenches, "Pollock and Bean" and "International Trench" had claimed many men and just the thought of a tour at "the Bluff" spread fear. The final open stretch from "The Bluff", across the dry Comines Canal bed to St.Eloi was held by the 26th (New Brunswick) and 25th (Nova Scotia) Battalions. Shelling was always severe and in a 24 hour period it was not unusual to receive one round every three minutes!

At 6:00 am on June 2nd, 1916 General Mercer and the 8th Brigade commander, Brigadier Victor Williams met with Lieut.-Colonel Ussher of the 4th CMR. They proceeded to Battalion Headquarters and then to the front lines on Mount Sorrel, arriving about 8:00 am. It was described as "a calm, beautiful and noticeably quiet morning". A few minutes later the German guns opened up with a ferocious bombardment that ripped the Canadian positions. Guns of all calibres fired on the 3rd Division's front. The heavy fire continued until the front line trenches and dugouts had been demolished and the bodies of shattered men lay strewn on the battlefield. Communication with the men in the front lines was cut-off. By early morning orders were given to the support troops to Stand To! At 1:00 pm the firing stopped, but there was no respite. The ground quivered and shook before exploding with the force of huge underground mines.

"It hurled into the air a large part of the (4th CMR)) front line and its defenders. Sandbags, wire, machine guns, bit of corrugated and bits of men were slung skyward."

With the firing of the mines large numbers of German infantry rose from their trenches and moved towards the remains of the Canadian front line. The Germans moved easily over the Canadian lines and passed quickly mopping up pockets of resistance put up by the few surviving men of the 1st and 4th CMR. The centre of the line had collapsed, but the flanks held out. The fire of the 5th Battalion on Hill 60 and the PPCLI in Sanctuary Wood, killed many attackers. However, the German objective was Observatory Ridge and it was quickly taken despite a gallant defence from the guns of the 5th Battery, Canadian Field Artillery. These "Suicide Guns" had fired over open sights at the advancing Germans, but to no avail. The crews paid with their lives. The Canadian support troops responded quickly and men of the 5th CMR in Maple Copse were quick to add to the counter-fire.

The Germans had torn a gap, 1,200 metres wide, in the centre of the Canadian line, from Mount Sorrel to Sanctuary Wood. They had overrun Tor Top, Mount Sorrel and advanced 600 metres along Observatory Ridge. In the face of heavy defending fire the Germans dug in.

In Sanctuary Wood the PPCLI had been driven from the front line trenches and were making a fighting retreat, trench block-by-trench block. The ferocious fighting continued throughout the afternoon. Men of the 42nd Battalion moved up to support the PPCLI. Lieutenant-Colonel Buller of the PPCLI personally led a group of men to help the others still clinging to the support and communication trenches running through Sanctuary Wood. Buller jumped on the parados to urge his men forward and was promptly shot dead.

By 3 pm the battle had subsided and reinforcements from the 3rd Division's 9th Brigade were moving up. But confusion still ruled at the H.Q. of the 3rd Division . They were unaware of the severity of the situation. Communication lines had been cut by the shelling and heavy artillery fire had prevented runners from getting through. Both Mercer and Williams were still missing, and it was not until later that they learned of their fates.

The Counter-attack, June 3rd, 1916

At Canadian Corps H.Q., General Byng ordered a counter-attack. The 1st Division was to attack the German positions on both sides of Observatory Ridge and the 3rd Division was to push the Germans out of Sanctuary Wood. Under the circumstances mounting such an attack, with all the confusion and the difficulties of moving fresh troops to the front, was asking a lot.

The 1st Division was to use four battalions in the attack. The 7th (British Columbia) and the 10th (Alberta) Battalions were to attack Mount Sorrel and the 15th (48th Highlanders of Toronto) and the 14th (Royal Montreal Regiment) Battalions were to push up both sides of Observatory Ridge. Originally scheduled to be a night attack it was 7 am before the attack was launched. Due to difficulties with the signal flares the attack of each battalion was launched separately. Against annihilating fire the men of the first wave were shot down. With no cover and in the graying dawn the attackers advanced, moving the line 500 metres forward. They failed to take their objectives but had succeeded in linking the Canadian lines at Maple Copse with those at Square Wood (behind Mount Sorrel), closing a 600 metre gap.

On the left flank the counter-attack was to involve three battalions of the 3rd Division. The 60th (Queen Victoria's Rifles), 52nd (New Ontario) and the 49th (Alberta) Battalions. However battlefield confusion and the inexperience of the 3rd Division resulted in only the 49th Battalion being properly assembled and prepared for the attack. To their credit they charged 300 metres into Sanctuary Wood and came very close to recapturing the old positions.

The counter-attack on June 3rd failed in its objectives but had succeeded in developing a better defensive line for the Canadians. It had been too hurried and did not have enough artillery support. These lessons were not missed by Julian Byng. Next time it would be different. Byng immediately started planning for another counter-attack, but bad weather conditions prevented aerial reconnaissance and he needed to obtain more artillery for the attack.

Over the next few days the 3rd Division was relieved by the 2nd Division. Men from the 28th (Saskatchewan) Battalion relieved the RCR at Hooge. The 31st (Alberta) Battalion supported them. The 24th (Queen Victoria's Rifles) and the 25th (Nova Scotia) Battalions relieved the 2nd (British Columbia) CMR and 5th CMR at Maple Copse. Both the 31st Battalion and the 43rd (Cameron Highlanders of Winnipeg) Battalions relieved the remnants of the PPCLI, 42nd and 49th Battalions in Sanctuary Wood. The 1st Division's 1st (Western Ontario) and 2nd (Eastern Ontario) Battalions now held the line from Hill 60 to Observatory Ridge.

Once relieved, the depleted battalions of the 3rd Division came out of the line and counted the losses. Their casualties were devastating. The PPCLI had lost 407 killed, wounded or prisoners, including their CO, Lieutenant-Colonel Herbert Buller. The 4th CMR had a staggering 626 casualties, including their CO, Lieutenant-Colonel Ussher, who was taken prisoner. The 1st CMR had lost their CO, Lieutenant-Colonel Alfred Shaw, killed near Tor Top. Two other COs were killed; Lieutenant-Colonel George Baker of the 5th CMR, and Lieut.-Colonel Archibald Hay of the 52nd Battalion. The RCR, who held the line at Hooge had 158 casualties. The other two battal-

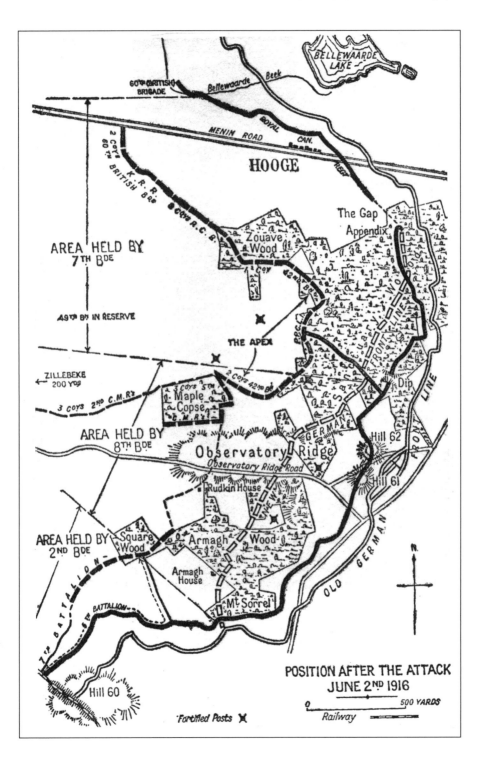

AREA HELD BY
7TH BDE

49TH BN IN RESERVE

AREA HELD BY
8TH BDE

AREA HELD BY
2ND BDE

BELLEWAARDE
LAKE

60TH BRITISH
BRIGADE

Bellewaarde Beek

2 COYS
60TH
BRITISH BDE

K.R.R.

8 COYS R.C.R.

MENIN ROAD

HOOGE

ROYAL CAN.

The Gap
Appendix

Zouave
Wood

4 COY

42 BN

THE APEX

2 COYS 42ND BN

ZILLEBEKE
← 200 YDS

3 COYS 2ND C.M.R.

3 COYS 5TH
Maple
Copse
C.M.R.

Observatory Ridge

Observatory Ridge Road

GERMAN

Hill 62

Dip

FRONT LINE

FRONT LINE

Rudkin House

Hill 61

Square
Wood

Armagh   Wood

Armagh
House

7TH BATTALION

8TH BATTALION

Mt Sorrel

OLD GERMAN

N.

Hill 60

Fortified Posts ✗

POSITION AFTER THE ATTACK
JUNE 2ND 1916

0   500 YARDS
Railway

ions in the 7th Brigade; the 42nd and 49th had 283 and 366 killed, wounded and taken prisoner respectively. To compound the losses it was later revealed that General Mercer had been killed by shell fire and that Brigadier-General Williams had been wounded and taken prisoner. During the entire war no other division suffered losses in men and senior officers comparable to those of the 3rd Division at Mount Sorrel.

Hooge, June 6th, 1916

On June 6th, 1916, two companies of the 28th (Saskatchewan) Battalion were holding the outpost positions at Hooge. Two other companies of the 28th were also holding the support trench 500 metres behind the front. At 3:05 pm the Germans fired a series of four mines under the outpost positions and literally obliterated one company (about 200 men) of the 28th Battalion. German infantry attacked and quickly captured the front lines at Hooge, but severe retaliatory fire by the other companies of the 28th and the 31st (Alberta) Battalion in Zouave Wood stopped them from advancing further. But the Germans were quite content with their gains and quickly dug-in.

The Counter-Attack, June 13th, 1916

The preparations for Byng's counter-attack were ready by June 12th, 1916. The artillery and the infantry were in place. More than 200 artillery pieces were concentrated to assist in the attack and between June 9th and 12th they pounded the German positions.

The plan was an auspicious one, a night attack planned for 2 am on June 13th, 1916. The attacking force was principally the 1st Division. The 3rd (Toronto Regiment) Battalion was to recapture Mount Sorrel, 500 metres from its jump-off line. To its left the 16th (Western Canadian Scottish) and the 13th (Black Watch of Montreal) Battalions would advance on each side of Observatory Ridge and capture Hill 62 (Tor Top). It would be an advance of 700 metres. The 58th (Central Ontario) Battalion of the 3rd Division would attack from positions on the edge of Sanctuary Wood and push into the Wood 300 metres and retake the old Canadian front lines.

Thomas Anderson Christie
Company Sergeant-Major
28th (Saskatchewan)
Battalion

Died of wounds June 8th, 1916. Born at Whithorn, Scotland, November 10th, 1889. Son of Andrew and Isabella Christie of Whithorn, Scotland.

Enlisted in the 28th Battalion on October 1914 at Broderick, Saskatchewan. Served in France from September 1915.

On June 6th, 1916 when in the trenches at Hooge, he was seriously wounded. Christie was immediately taken to a Casualty Clearing Station, where he died of his wounds. Buried in Lijssenthoek Military Cemetery, Belgium.

John Carron Sime
Private
24th (Victoria's Rifles)
Battalion

Killed in action June 7th, 1916. Born at Crail, Fife, Scotland, in September 1892. Son of James and Catherine Sime of Fife, Scotland.

Enlisted at Montreal in the 24th Battalion in October 1914. Served in France from September 1915. On the night of June 7th, 1916 his unit was moving through Zillebeke to reinforce the front. They were beside the church when an enemy shell exploded amongst his section, killing Private Sime and many others. Buried in Zillebeke Churchyard, Belgium.

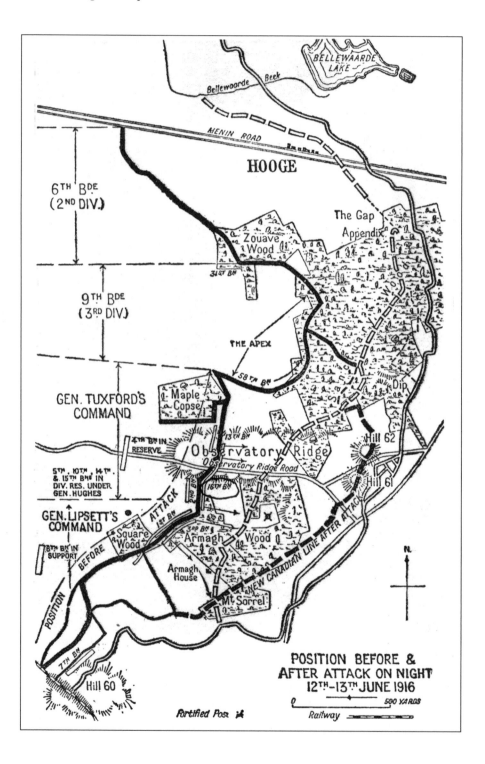

BELLEWAARDE LAKE

Bellewaarde Beek

MENIN ROAD

HOOGE

6TH BDE (2ND DIV.)

The Gap
Appendix

Zouave Wood

31ST BN

9TH BDE (3RD DIV)

THE APEX

58TH BN

GEN. TUXFORD'S COMMAND

Maple Copse

4TH BN IN RESERVE

13TH BN

Observatory Ridge

Observatory Ridge Road

Hill 62

5TH, 10TH, 14TH & 15TH BNS IN DIV. RES. UNDER GEN. HUGHES.

16TH BN

Hill 61

GEN. LIPSETT'S COMMAND

8TH BN IN SUPPORT

ATTACK

1ST BN

2ND BN

3RD BN

Square Wood

Armagh Wood

NEW CANADIAN LINE AFTER ATTACK

N

Armagh House

POSITION BEFORE

Mt Sorrel

7TH BN

Hill 60

POSITION BEFORE & AFTER ATTACK ON NIGHT 12TH-13TH JUNE 1916

0 — 500 YARDS

Fortified Post

Railway

Like all well-planned and well-executed battles there is little to say but that they were successful. The effective artillery fire demolished all German opposition and the Canadians quickly advanced and recaptured most of what was lost on June 2nd, 1916. The Germans, in return, pounded their lost positions throughout June 13th/14th. The Canadians dug in to save themselves, but still suffered many casualties. It was clear the Germans were not going to contest this last Canadian attack. The Battle of Mount Sorrel was over.

The Canadian Corps had lost 8,000 men killed, wounded and 536 prisoners. They had lost two Generals and six Battalion COs (Lieutenant-Colonel Creighton of the 1st Battalion was mortally wounded on June 13th) killed or taken prisoner. For these heavy losses they had only regained the basic territory they had previously lost. However this was an important turning point for the Canadian Corps. Under adverse conditions they had recovered from a severe defeat and methodically planned and executed a difficult night attack to regain, not only the lost ground, but their lost confidence. This recovery was directly related to their new commander, Julian Byng, and it was a sign of things to come.

The Canadian Corps remained in the Ypres Salient throughout the summer of 1916. It was always dangerous and in those two months they lost another 1,000 men killed. At the end of August 1916 they were ordered south to participate in the great Somme Offensive. The Canadian Corps would not return to the Salient until October 1917 when, in a four week period, they would capture the Passchendaele Ridge and suffer 16,000 casualties.

Throughout the war the Canadians spent less than six months around Ypres, but had more than 16,000 killed there. The deadly Salient accounted for more than 25% of all Canadian deaths in the Great War.

Tour Itinerary (Duration 3.5 hours)

Point 1: Ypres Ramparts; The Southern Sector of the Salient

Point 2: Hill 62; The Attack on Hill 62, June 2nd, 1916

Point 3: Maple Copse and Observatory Ridge

Point 4: Mount Sorrel

Point 5: Sanctuary Wood; June 2nd, 1916

Point 6: Hooge; June 6th, 1916

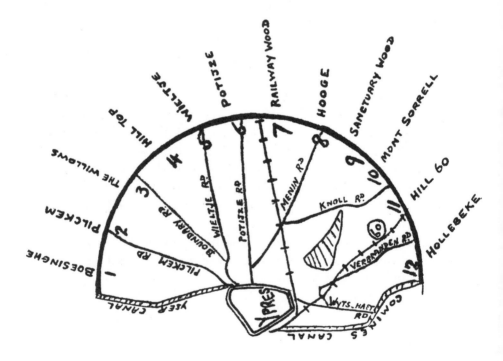

The Sectors of the Salient.

The Battle of Mount Sorrel, June 1916

The Tour

In the text I have used the French names of the towns and villages as they were in the First World War. Today the names reflect their Flemish origins. Please refer to the listing of "Modern" and "1914-1918" spellings in the "About Ypres" section at the beginning of this book.

The tour starts with an orientation to the Ypres Salient. Park your car in the Grote Markt in Ypres and walk 200 metres east to the impressive Menin Gate Memorial. Walk through the arch into the Memorial and mid-way turn right and climb the stairs to the loggia. When you reach the top you will be standing on the ramparts. Keep walking south along the ramparts. It is a pleasant walk along a pretty pathway. The southern sector of the Ypres Salient is off to your left (refer to Sectors of the Salient). Unfortunately the trees block most of the view, at the best the view is poor so you will have to use your imagination to bring back the events of 1916. After 800 metres you reach the south-east corner of the walls. You can continue on to the Lille Gate, 100 metres to the west. (A few metres on is the beautiful Ramparts (Lille Gate) Cemetery.)

Point 1: Ypres Ramparts; The Southern Sector of the Salient

Hundreds of Canadian soldiers and their Headquarters were dug into the safe walls of the ramparts beneath you. It was from here that the attack was observed and the orders to reinforce and counter-attack given. It is not hard to imagine the confusion in a battle of this nature where all communication to the front was cut, and entire staffs were missing. From the Lille Gate you can see the southern sector of the Ypres Salient, 1914- 1918. To get a better view, walk down and follow the main road south until the signs to Kemmel and Zillebeke. This is the infamous Shrapnel Corner. The first thing you notice is how undistinguished the land is. There seems to be no discernible features, only some rolling woodland some four km away, running to the east and south-east. A slight, tree-covered ridge can be seen. It is amongst these trees that the Battle of Mount Sorrel was fought. The

Salient in 1916 was still recognizable as a "civilized" place but by the end of the battle most of the trees on the ridge would have been destroyed.

The front lines ran in a three km, south-westerly arc starting at Hooge and ending at Hill 60. Four km east-south-est is Hill 62. Hill 60 is 3.5 km south-east of where you stand. On June 2nd, 1916 the entire arc was lit-up in a cascade of artllery fire and smoke. The Battle of Mount Sorrel had begun.

Walk back to the Menin Gate on the Ramparts and return to your car. Exit the town on the east (Ypres is constantly changing its road systems so pay attention to the signs), following road signs to Menin (Menen). Follow the road (N8) and watch for signs for the Hill 62 Canadian Battlefield Memorial. After three km turn right on the road leading 1.5 km to the Memorial.

You are driving over the fields on which the Canadians counter-attacked late June 2nd and on June 3rd. Hooge and Hooge Crater Cemetery can clearly be seen on your left. (You can imagine the 28th Battalion companies being mined and blown to smithereens on June 6th, 1916.) It is easy to see why the commanding position of Hooge was so important to both sides. Drive by the Sanctuary Wood Museum (worth a visit, as many of the Canadians support trenches have been preserved, as well as a great number of battlefield artifacts) to the parking lot for the Hill 62 Memorial. Park your car and walk up to the Memorial. It is one of the six "sugar cube" memorials erected by Canada after the war. These unimaginative pieces of art commemorate Canada's most bloody battles of the First World War.

Ypres strongholds in ancient city walls used as modern H.Q. April-May 1919

(PUBLIC ARCHIVES OF CANADA PA 4492)

George Harold Baker
Lieutenant-Colonel
5th Canadian Mounted Rifles

Died of wounds June 3rd, 1916. Born at Sweetsburg, Quebec, November 4th, 1877. He was the son of Jane Cowan Baker and Senator G.B. Baker. Served as a Member of Parliament in Ottawa. Commissioned at Montreal, Quebec as the Commanding Officer of the 5th CMR. Went to France in October 1915.

During the heavy fighting at Maple Copse on June 2nd he was struck in the chest by a shell fragment, and fell unconscious. He was taken to a dressing station and died shortly after midnight. Buried in Poperinghe New Military Cemetery, Belgium.

Harvey Watt Cockshutt
Lieutenant
4th Canadian Mounted Rifles

Died of wounds as a Prisoner-of-War, June 2nd, 1916. Born at Brantford, Ontario, November 22nd, 1883. He was commissioned in Toronto as an original officer of the 4th CMR. Went to France in October 1915. In the German assault on Mount Sorrel he was in the front line trenches. After the battle he was listed as missing, presumed dead. In 1919 his grave was found in Wervicq Road German Cemetery, indicating he had died as a Prisoner-of-War. His body was exhumed and re-interred in Zantvoorde British Cemetery, Belgium.

Point 2: Hill 62; The Attack on Hill 62, June 2nd, 1916

Make your way past the Monument, through the shrubberies to the eastern side of the park, overlooking a small farm. You are standing where the front lines of the 1st Canadian Mounted Rifles were on June 2nd, 1916. The German lines were at the bottom of the hill. From here the Canadians could see significant movements of German troops, a clear sign that an attack was imminent.

Looking south-west, following the tree lines, 1 km away is Mount Sorrel. On June 2nd it was held by the 4th CMR, a sister battalion of the 1st CMR. When the German barrage intensified and the full weight of the German artillery focussed on the line from Hill 62 to Mount Sorrel this entire front disappeared in a cloud of smoke and fire. This crushing barrage was followed by the explosion of underground mines and with this additional force the Germans had succeeded in obliterating the front line positions. Imagine, after the quavering of the land had stilled, German infantry walking up the slope before you, killing or capturing the surviving Canadians. To the south, fields of field-gray uniformed soldiers were patiently moving across No Man's Land, taking over positions, and rounding up shell-shocked prisoners. By capturing the high points overlooking Ypres the Germans had accomplished their objective.

Return to "the cube", turn left (west) and walk over to the observation alcove.

From here you can see the spires of Ypres, Maple Copse (the entrance to the Maple Copse Cemetery can also be seen), and on your left a somewhat obscured Observatory Ridge. After successfully capturing the front lines the Germans advanced across these fields. Mid-way between you and Maple Copse the "Sacrifice Guns" of the Canadian Field Artillery fired over open sights at the enemy. The crews of the batteries fought to the last man. For the only time in the war Canadian guns were captured by the Germans. To their credit the Canadian troops (5th CMR) in Maple Copse stood their ground and poured fire into the advancing Germans, inflicting heavy casualties.

The German infantry seemed reluctant to close up with the Canadians and let their artillery do the killing. The 5th CMR

View from Hill 62 to Mount Sorrel.

(N. CHRISTIE)

View from Point 2, Maple Copse is on the right, spires of Ypres, mid horizon.

(N. CHRISTIE)

suffered terribly from the shelling on June2nd/3rd, and amongst the fallen was their Commanding Officer, Lieutenant-Colonel Harold Baker, MP. Baker was struck in the chest by a shell fragment and died shortly afterwards. He is buried in Poperinghe New Military Cemetery, Plot II Row G Grave 1.

Hidden from view by the trees on your left are the fields over which the 1st Division counter-attacked on June 3rd, 1916. They will be discussed in Point 3.

Over the next few days there was no substantial fighting in this area. Shelling was heavy and deadly, but between June 4th and June 13th both sides improved their positions. No doubt the Germans thought their gains were secure. No doubt the Canadians thought they were not. Under their new Commander, General Byng, the Canadians planned and waited for their opportunity. On the evening of June 12th weather conditions improved, artillery preparations were complete and the infantry was set. Launching the attack at 1:30 am, in total darkness the men of the 13th (Black Watch of Montreal) and 16th (Western Canadian Scottish) Battalions advanced across these fields, up Hill 62 and regained the summit. It was an incredible achievement, but also a costly one; the 13th had more than 300 casualties and the 16th Battalion had 269 killed, wounded and missing.

By June 14th, 1916 the shattered remnants of Hill 62 were back in Canadian hands. The Germans had no taste left for the fight but their big guns punished the victors and most casualties were a result of the German artillery fire. Losses in the infantry assault had been light.

Walk back to the front of the Memorial and stop at the top of the steps.

Looking into the wood, Sanctuary Wood, on your right it is hard to imagine the severity of the fighting that took place there between the remnants of the 1st CMR and the Würtembergers. There was an elaborate system of support and communication trenches in the wood and it is from their reserve positions that the 1st CMR held up the Germans. (It was also true the Germans were less interested in this area as it was overlooked by Hooge and Hill 62.) The 1st CMR lost their CO, Lieutenant-Colonel

A.E. Shaw, who was killed in the action. His body was never recovered and he is commemorated by name only on the Menin Gate Memorial.

The 1st CMR were reinforced by brave parties of men of the 3rd Division: the 43rd (Cameron Highlanders of Winnipeg), 49th (Alberta), 52nd (Northern Ontario) and 42nd (Black Watch of Montreal) Battalions all pushed their men forward, through heavy fire, to reinforce the line between June 2nd to the 4th.

This area of the wood was recaptured June 13th, 1916 by the 58th (Central Ontario) Battalion.

Return to your car and drive back to the Menin Road (N8). It is worth a stop at Sanctuary Wood Cemetery. Go to the back of this triangle-shaped cemetery and stand up on the stone bench. Looking west you can see Maple Copse and Observatory Ridge, the scene of the fiercest fighting in the Battle of Mount Sorrel.

Turn left going back to Ypres. After 1.2 km (past Birr Crossroads Cemetery), turn left on the road to Zillebeke. (This is the infamous Hell-fire Corner).

Four hundred metres from Hell-fire Corner, towards Zillebeke corner, is where the "China Wall" communication trench crossed the road leading to the front line. The building at this corner was known as Gordon House and it was here Captain Blackader received his mortal wound. It was an important collection post for men moving to and from the front. (See "The Mystery of Captain Blackader" on page 87)

Continue on past Perth (China Wall) Cemetery into the village of Zillbeke. You can stop in front of the Church and check out the Churchyard. From the back of the cemetery there is an excellent view of Maple Copse and you can see Sanctuary Wood Cemetery.

Shortly after the church the road comes to a "T" junction, turn left and just at the edge of the village turn left again following signs to Maple Copse Cemetery. (At this turn-off General Williams' 8th Brigade Headquarters was located). The road leads past "Valley Cottages" (400 metres), up Observatory Ridge. After 1 km the left turn-off to Maple Copse Cemetery is reached. Pull off to the side of the road and get out of your car.

THE HILL 62 CANADIAN MEMORIAL

The Canadian monument on Hill 62 (Tor Top), south-east of the City of Ypres, stands on one of eight First World War Canadian battlefields officially commemorated.

In 1920, the Canadian Battlefield Monument Commission decided to erect memorials at:

St. Julien - to commemorate the Second Battle of Ypres

Hill 62 - to commemorate the Battle of Mount Sorrel and St.Eloi Craters

Courcelette - to commemorate the Battle of the Somme

Vimy - to commemorate the Battle of Vimy Ridge

Passchendaele - to commemorate the Battle of Passchendaele

Le Quesnel - to commemorate the Battle of Amiens

Dury - to commemorate the Battle of Arras 1918 and the capture of the Drocourt- Queant line

Bourlon Wood - to commemorate the Battles of the Canal du Nord, Cambrai, the capture of Valenciennes and Mons and the March to the Rhine

It was decided that Vimy would act as the National Memorial and have a unique design. The other seven would be marked with identical memorials. A competition was held to choose an architect to design the monuments. Walter Allward of Toronto was chosen for Vimy's unique memorial and Frederick C. Clemesha of Regina took second place. Clemesha's design, "The Brooding Soldier," was built at St. Julien and had such a stark effect at its unveiling in 1923 that the Monument Commission decided it also should remain unique.

In conjunction with the architectural advisor, P. E. Nobbs, the cube design was developed for the remaining six monuments. A 13-tonne block of Stanstead granite was used for each. A wreath was carved into two sides of the monument and on the other two sides was engraved a brief explanation of the exploits of the Canadian Corps in that specific battle. One side is in English, the other in French.

At Hill 62, the monument reads:

HERE AT MOUNT SORREL AND ON THE LINE FROM HOOGE TO ST. ELOI THE CANADIAN CORPS FOUGHT IN DEFENCE OF YPRES APRIL-AUGUST 1916.

Around the base of the stone, it reads:

HONOUR TO CANADIANS WHO ON THE FIELDS OF FLANDERS AND OF FRANCE FOUGHT IN THE CAUSE OF THE ALLIES WITH SACRIFICE AND DEVOTION

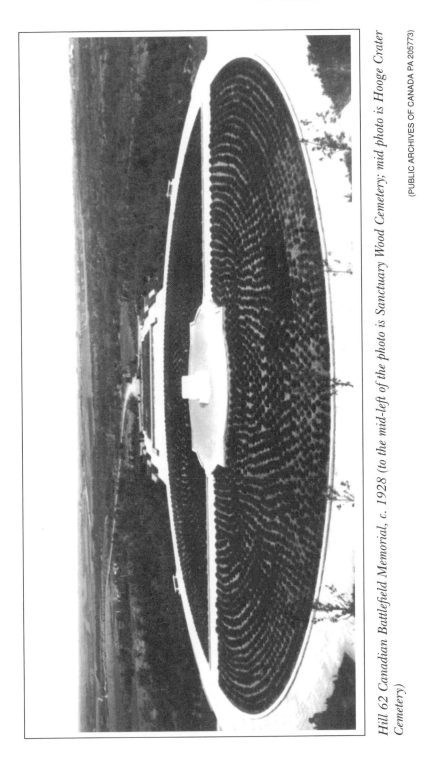

Hill 62 Canadian Battlefield Memorial, c. 1928 (to the mid-left of the photo is Sanctuary Wood Cemetery; mid photo is Hooge Crater Cemetery)

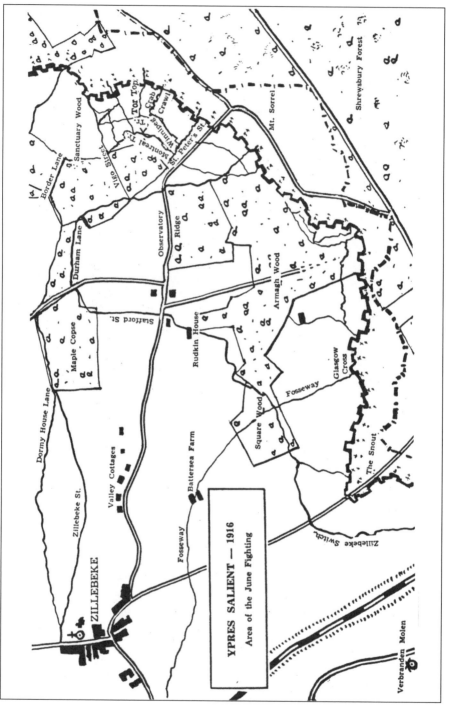

YPRES SALIENT — 1916

Area of the June Fighting

Zillebeke village, April-May 1919

(PUBLIC ARCHIVES OF CANADA C 4592)

Point 3: Maple Copse and Observatory Ridge.

You are standing on the western toe of Observatory Ridge. This tongue of land running east-west overlooks the entire Canadian line from Hooge to Hill 60. German possession of the Ridge would make the Canadian positions untenable and probably force a withdrawal from the southern sector of the Ypres Salient. Thus Observatory Ridge was the main objective of the Germans, and the scene of the fiercest fighting of the battle.

To orient yourself; Maple Copse is the wood 300 metres north of you, Hill 62 (the Canadian Memorial) is 600 metres east-north-east, and the Canadian lines on Mount Sorrel are 600 metres south.

After the concentrated bombardment the Germans easily advanced over the front lines from Mount Sorrel to Hill 62. It was not until they reached this position that they came under severe fire from the 5th CMR in Maple Copse, and from the 5th (Saskatchewan) Battalion holding Hill 60, 1,100 metres south-west of you. The 7th (British Columbia) Battalion fired on the attackers from support trenches behind Hill 60.

Just north of the road and 200 metres to the east was the location of the heroic stand of the "Sacrifice Guns". The gun crews were killed defending the guns. Among those killed was Lieutenant Charles Penner Cotton, son of Major-General Cotton. His brother, Captain Ross Penner was killed June 13th in the counter-attack on Hill 62. They are both buried in Lijssenthoek Military Cemetery.

When night fell the Germans started to dig in and prepare their defences against any counter-attacks. In the meantime men of the 1st Division were ordered forward to recapture Observatory Ridge. On the morning of June 3rd four battalions attacked the Germans. The 10th (Alberta) and 7th (British Columbia) Battalions attacked in a south-easterly direction from the support trenches behind Hill 60 towards Mount Sorrel.

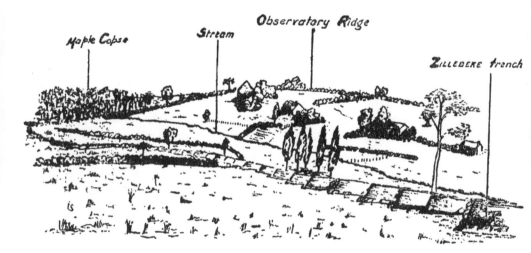

Valley Cottages from Zillebeke

Without adequate preparation and proper artillery support their attack was doomed and the men were shot down. Despite the heavy casualties there was little gain. Their attack took place across the open fields 500 metres south-west of where you stand.

The other two attacking battalions: the 14th (Royal Montreal Regiment) and the 15th (48th Highlanders of Toronto) attacked, north and south respectively, of the road you are standing by. In the face of heavy fire they pushed forward. The Battalions advanced 500 metres before being driven back, but they gained 300 metres and dug in. They built a 700 metre long defensive position linking the existing defences in Maple Copse with the support trenches behind Hill 60.

After the attacks of June 3rd the gap created by the German offensive had been sealed. Where you are standing is 100 metres east of the new Canadian line and only 300 metres from the German lines.

The positions remained stable for the next 10 days. Then at 1:30 am on June 13th, 1916, in pitch darkness, four other battalions of the 1st Division struck the Germans with such surprise that they regained the old Canadian lines with few casualties. The 3rd (Toronto Regiment) and 1st (Western Ontario) Battalions recaptured Mount Sorrel. The 16th and 13th Battalions attacked Observatory Ridge, through the place where you are now standing. They swept up Observatory Ridge and recaptured all the ground from Hill 62 to Mount Sorrel. It was a resounding success.

The Germans never really contested the Canadian victory. Their artillery pounded the front causing many casualties, but the outcome of the battle was never in doubt.

Return to your car and continue up Observatory Ridge until the road hits a 'T' junction. Turn right and drive 600 metres. When you reach a small farmhouse on your left, stop your car and get out. (The road over which you have just driven was known as "Green Jacket Ride").

Point 4: Mount Sorrel

Looking west the small, wooded hillock in front of you is Mount Sorrel. Looking back along Green Jacket Ride, Hill 62 is

View from Mount Sorrel. The smoke in the mid-distance is Hill 62.

(N. CHRISTIE)

visible one km north. (You may want to use binoculars for this view. Look for the farm house just outside the Canadian Park). The German trenches prior to and after the battle ran close to this road.

On June 2nd, 1916 the General Commanding the 3rd Division, the Brigadier and the CO of the Battalion in the line, the 4th CMR, were reconnoitring the defences near Mount Sorrel when all hell broke loose. In the ensuing bombardment they sought refuge in the safe dugouts in the support trenches behind Mount Sorrel. Trapped by the shelling their situation became desperate when the Germans launched their attack.

The Germans left their trenches where you are standing and stormed up the hill capturing or killing any shocked survivors of the 4th CMR they stumbled upon. What they did not know was just over the hill, 300 metres from where you are standing, were two Canadian Generals, trapped like rats, with no way of escaping the swarming German infantry. It was a success beyond their

Mount Sorrel

wildest expectations.

Unfortunately, Mount Sorrel and the area around it is private property and any access to it requires the permission of the local farmer. So for this tour you will have to imagine the plight of Generals Mercer and Williams.

The German advance was so quick and their barrage so concentrated that when General Mercer tried to make his way back he was killed by a shell fragment. Brigadier Victor Williams was wounded and taken prisoner, as was Lieutenant-Colonel Ussher of the 4th CMR. They were the three highest ranking Canadians captured in the war. Brigadier-General Williams was one only eight British (Commonwealth) Generals captured on the Western Front during the entire war!

After the Germans captured Mount Sorrel on June 2nd the position was never under threat of attack, although Canadian and British artillery hammered the newly dug German trenches, until June 13th.

Byng's staff, however, was planning a surprise for the Germans. They had the infantry reserves for an attack, but needed to get the artillery ready. To do so would require a thorough examination of aerial photographs that would allow the heavy guns to register on enemy targets (due to cloud cover preventing effective aerial reconnaissance the attack had been delayed). The Canadians were ready to attack on the night of June 12th/13th, 1916. As with the attack on Hill 62, the recapture of Mount Sorrel was accomplished with relative ease by the 3rd Battalion with assistance from the 1st. The Germans made a couple of feeble attempts to regain the hill but artillery quickly dispensed the attackers.

The chief cause of casualties was the deadly fire of the guns. For example the 3rd Battalion easily retook Mount Sorrel with few casualties, but after 36 hours holding the new line they had suffered 415 casualties, including 137 dead! The 1st Battalion lost its CO in the counter-attack, when Lieutenant-Colonel Creighton was mortally wounded by a shell. He died two days later and was buried in Lijssenthoek Military Cemetery.

Return to your car and turn around and head back along Green Jacket Ride. (To visit Hill 60 Memorial Park continue straight ahead on the road to a 'T' junction and turn right. After 600 metres turn left to visit the Park.) Drive past the turn-off to Observatory Ridge, and the Hill 62 Canadian Memorial. After 1.5 km you will reach an access road on your left, pull over and get out of your car.

Point 5: Sanctuary Wood; June 2nd, 1916

You are actually standing 300 metres behind the German lines. The large wood on your left is Sanctuary Wood. The small wood on the right contained the major German defensive works known as "Stirling Castle" and the "Birdcage". These positions commanded the Canadian lines that ran through Sanctuary Wood. In the wood the PPCLI (Princess Patricia's Canadian Light Infantry) occupied a complex series of support and firing trenches that provided a deep zone of defence. The front line positions in the wood were 400 metres east of you. The largest ones were known as "The Loop", and "The Appendix", and held

The Fate of General Mercer

"After a time the fire slackened and Mercer, who had miraculously escaped injury, determined to push his way back to his headquarters to organize resistance to the attack that the enemy would inevitably put over. He was still feeling the effects of the shock he had received, and as he went towards the rear just before one o'clock, he had to be supported by Gooderham (Mercer's A.D.C.). The communications trenches had all been obliterated, and in this trip, made overland, there was but little shelter to be gained. Just as they reached Armagh Wood a chance shot hit Mercer in the leg, breaking a bone. His aide dragged him into a nearby ditch and did everything in his power to ease his suffering. Shortly after this event the bombardment lifted over Armagh Wood, and the Huns swarmed through the 4th Canadian Mounted Rifles. During the night eight attempts were made to recover the lost ground. While the fourth attack was on, a British shell burst close to Mercer and a piece of shrapnel pierced his heart. Gooderham, who had gallantly stood by him until this moment, remained alone in no-man's-land until the morning of 4 June, when he was found by the Germans and taken prisoner." (Taken from "Canada in the Great World War", Volume III; The United Publishers of Canada, 1919.)

Grave of Major-General Malcolm S. Mercer, Lijssenthoek Military Cemetery, Belgium.

two companies of the PPCLI. It was against these men the Germans concentrated their fire and launched their assault on June 2nd, 1916.

Unfortunately Sanctuary Wood is private land so, as at Mount Sorrel, you will have to imagine the defence of the wood. One of the soldiers anticipating the German attack was my Great Uncle, Sergeant John Christie. Uncle John had enlisted in the 4th University Company (this is the closest he ever came to a university) in Montreal in 1915. He joined the PPCLI in the field in April 1916. This was to be his first battle.

During the morning of June 2nd, 1916 German artillery fire began pounding the Canadian front line. Over the next several hours the concentration of gun-fire escalated. Finally the German infantry attacked using flame-throwers and as at Mount Sorrel and Hill 62 the front lines were quickly captured and their garrisons killed.

The ensuing battle for the Wood was a ferocious struggle. Fighting against overwhelming numbers the PPCLI fought from trench to trench always extracting a toll from the enemy before a short retirement to continue the fight from another post.

The remnants of the original companies held the Germans at a support trench near the western edge of Sanctuary Wood. It was critical this trench "Warrington Avenue" was held as it prevented the Germans from linking up their attacks. It was in "Warrington Avenue" that Lieutenant-Colonel Buller organized his men and through sheer courage slowed the German advance. Buller rallied his men and to direct fire on the approaching Germans, stood on the parados. He was killed almost instantly.

After the battle Buller's body was removed and laid to rest in Voormezeele Enclosure No. 3, the PPCLI Regimental Cemetery. He is buried beside the PPCLI's first CO, Lieutenant-Colonel Farquhar, who was killed by a sniper in 1915.*

Well beyond our view, on the other side of the wood, men of the 42nd (Black Watch of Montreal) and 49th (Alberta) Battalions were coming to the aid of the surviving Patricias. On June 3rd the PPCLI positions near the Menin Road were

---

*see; *"With the Patricia's in Flanders - Then and Now"* by Captain S.K. Newman.

deemed untenable and they withdrew to the support positions. Activity in this sector quieted down, and it was not until June 13th that the 58th (Central Ontario) Battalion recaptured some of the old positions in Sanctuary Wood. The remaining territory would remain in German hands until the Allied offensive in July 1917.

Sanctuary Wood was a tremendous battle for the PPCLI. They suffered 407 casualties including 187 dead. Fortunately Uncle John survived the struggle unscathed. It is remarkable that in May 1915 less than 600 metres north-east of Sanctuary Wood, at Bellewaerde, the PPCLI suffered 392 casualties! They would return a third time to the Ypres Salient in October 1917 and suffer a further 363 casualties. Can there be any wonder why the PPCLI has more men listed on the Menin Gate Memorial than any other Canadian Battalion?

Return to your car and continue on the road until you meet the 'T' junction in the Menin Road. Turn (known as Clapham Junction) left and drive past the Bellewaarde Amusement Park (talk about ironic). After 1.3 km you reach the hamlet of Hooge ('t Hoge). Stop at the Hooge Chapel (where the Pope once gave a sermon), and get out of your car. Walk across the road to Hooge Crater Cemetery.

Point 6: Hooge; June 6th, 1916

Hooge was the scene of fierce fighting in 1915. During the first days of the Battle of Mount Sorrel it was lightly involved, but it was the centre of the fighting on June 6th. Each date will be treated at separate ends of the cemetery.

Walk to the back of the cemetery.

The situation on June 2nd, 1916 was: the Royal Canadian Regiment held the left flank of the Canadian Corps from a point 500 metres north-west of Hooge. Their positions ran through heavily cratered ground just on the other side of the chapel, running through the hamlet, to a point 150 metres south of the Menin Road. On their right flank there was a stretch of 300 metres, known as "the Gap" that was unmanned. The RCR had half their men in the front lines north and south of Hooge. The other half were in support trenches, 200 metres west of you. You

"HIS NOBLE SACRIFICE"

12th June 1916

Dear Lady Buller,

Had it been possible, I would have written you before. I realize the loss which the Regiment has sustained in our beloved Colonel, can in no way be compared with what it means to you of whom he had so often spoken to me. The Regiment which he loved so well, and led so gallantly, suffered tremendous losses on the 1st, 2nd, 3rd and 4th of June, six of his officers being killed and 15 either wounded or missing and of the latter I fear there is little chance of their being ever heard from again.

Lt.-Col. H.C. Buller

It was on the Second of June when the enemy had entered our front line in considerable force and were bombing down on our right, that he personally ordered a counter flanking attack which proved successful and was at the time kneeling on the parados that he was hit through the heart by a bullet. The Medical Officer of the Regiment was beside him and he assures me that his noble sacrifice was without pain. We were heavily attacked all June the second and third and regained the ground on the fourth. Sergeant Cooper and eight men were selected from very many volunteers and at night on the fifth we placed Henry in the same grave as Colonel Farquhar whom he loved so well, with the remnant of the old original Regiment they formed and commanded, whose numbers now are very few, present to pay their last tribute of respect. I know that every man in the Regiment feels that he has lost a personal friend, whose only object was to increase the proficiency of the Regiment as a fighting unit and understand his men, which he most thoroughly did.

May I distribute among his officers and a few of the old original N.C.O.s some of his few personal belongings which I know would be greatly prized - if this is not your wish, please tell me so.

There is nothing further that I can say, the Regiment is staggered at its loss, and is determined to follow the high standard set as and whenever the opportunity occurs to try and pay some part of the debt we owe.

The Regiment, which is reduced to three hundred fighting men, has asked me to send you their deepest sympathy and to be allowed to share with you your grief.

Agar Adamson, Major

are roughly mid-way between the front line trenches and the support trenches. Looking to the east you can see Sanctuary Wood; to the south-east 1.5 km, not visible through the trees, is Hill 62 (you can see Sanctuary Wood Cemetery); and 1.7 km south, again obscured by the trees, is Mount Sorrel. The spires of Ypres can be seen four km to the west.

On June 2nd German artillery blasted the Canadian positions from Sanctuary Wood (PPCLI) along the arc to Mount Sorrel, obliterating what remained of the forests, destroying the defensive positions and inflicting heavy casualties. The German infantry then advanced over the trenches. The breakthrough at Observatory Ridge, between Hill 62 and Mount Sorrel, must have unnerved the RCRs in the trenches, however they held firm, and waited.

Later in the afternoon the Germans attacked the RCR positions at Hooge but in a short and furious fight were driven back. Shelling continued intermittently until the next day, June 3rd. The German advance in Sanctuary Wood (Point 5) had forced the PPCLI to fall back from their positions south of 'the Gap'. This withdrawal had left the flank of the RCR open, but fortunately the Germans did not attack. It seems that they had other plans for the garrison at Hooge.

While the RCR were holding the line at Hooge, reinforcements from the 42nd Battalion were crossing the field to the south of you, quickly moving through heavy shell fire, to assist the surviving PPCLI in the support trenches on the fringe of the western side of Sanctuary Wood.

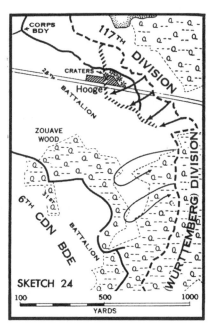

The Attack on Hooge, June 6th, 1916.

(DND)

As we had seen in Point 3, on June 3rd, 1916 the 1st Division had made a costly counter-attack on the Germans on Observatory Ridge. It had had some success. The counter-attack was supposed to include a simultaneous attack on Sanctuary Wood by three battalions of the 3rd Division. However the German artillery, heavy traffic in the communication trenches and general inexperience and confusion resulted in only one battalion being in place for the counter-attack!

Even though the 49th (Alberta) Battalion was the only one in the line, at 7:00 am on June 3rd, 1916, they courageously attacked. In the field south of you the Albertans were greeted by enemy fire and many men fell. To their credit they continued their advance, men falling and stumbling forward through the rain of German machine-gun bullets and entered the German-held trenches. In fierce fighting the Germans were pushed back and the 49th established a position inside Sanctuary Wood. Their losses were terrible. For the advance of 800 metres 356 were killed or wounded.

The lines opposite the northern part of Sanctuary Wood remained the same for the rest of the battle. In fact it was only in the northern part of Sanctuary Wood and at Hooge (to be discussed below) that the Canadians failed to retake their original positions. The RCR were relieved in the early morning on June 6th, 1916 by the 28th (Saskatchewan) Battalion of the 2nd Division. Even though the RCR were only holding the line, they suffered 158 casualties.

Walk back to the entrance of the cemetery.

The 28th had been in France since September 1915 and had been involved in the bloody and confused fighting at St. Eloi Craters in April 1916. When they took over the trenches the sector had been relatively quiet for a few days. The 31st (Alberta) Battalion supported the 28th in the trenches 500 metres behind them, parallel to the front line,.

At 3:05 pm on June 6th, 1916, 200 metres of the 28th's front was blasted by the explosion of four German underground mines. Two companies of the 28th Battalion were destroyed and German infantry quickly captured Hooge but failed to advance to the support trenches. The Germans had captured what they wanted - Hooge.

The mine explosions took place 200 metres north-east of you, on the other side of the Chapel in the Chateau Grounds (private property). The loss of Hooge by the Canadians must have created a certain distain from British troops. Holding Hooge was a point of honour and they had suffered so much holding the shattered hamlet.

The Battle of Mount Sorrel marked the second time the Ypres Salient had extracted a mighty toll of Canadian lives. Over the summer 1,000 more Canadians would die in defence of Ypres. In August 1916 the Canadian Corps was moved to the Somme and later to the Vimy front. They would return to Ypres for a month in autumn 1917 when once again they would die by the thousands in the Salient. The only difference would be the location. This time it would be at Passchendaele.

Mount Sorrel was not a victory. In fact the Germans inflicted greater casualties on the Canadians than they incurred, so by First World War standards it was a German success. The battle was, however, a turning point in the development of the Canadian fighting machine. After the debacle of St. Eloi Craters the men had suffered a loss of confidence, both in themselves and their leaders. Mount Sorrel had restored some of that pride, and gave them confidence in the abilities of their new commander, Julian Byng. The men came to trust him and to follow his methods, knowing he had their interests at heart. Byng would mould those men into a force so strong that within 10 months they would attack and capture the strongest German position on the Western front, Vimy Ridge.

Return to your car and continue west on the Menin Road to Ypres. (A visit to the excellent museum at Hooge is worthwhile.)

George Samuel Tucker
Sergeant
3rd Battalion-Toronto Regiment
Killed in action June 13th, 1916.
Born at Palmetto Grove, Bermuda, July 17th, 1893. Son of Archdeacon George Tucker of Palmetto Grove, Bermuda.
Enlisted at Montreal in the 23rd Battalion in 1914. Joined the 3rd Battalion in France in 1915.
On the night of June 13th, 1916 he participated in the successful attack on Mount Sorrel. Sadly, Sergent Tucker was one of 137 men killed or missing in the attack of the 3rd Battalion.
He has no known grave and is commemorated on the Menin Gate Memorial.

George William Fraser
Sergeant
16th Battalion-Canadian Scottish
Killed in action June 13th, 1916.
Born in Fermoy, Ireland, December 9th. 1891. Son of John Fraser.
Enlisted at Winnipeg in the 16th Battalion in August 1914.
Served in France from February 1915. Fraser was killed in action on the night of June 13th, 1916 in the capture of Observatory Ridge. His body was recovered after the battle and buried in Railway Dugout Burial Ground, Zillebeke, Belgium.
His younger brother, an officer in the Royal Air Force was also killed in the war.

Cemeteries and Memorials
The Battle of Mount Sorrel, June 1916

The Ypres Salient is the largest cemetery in the world. For four years the armies of Britain, France and Germany waged a relentless battle, using every conceivable weapon of war, to dislodge an enemy from a piece of land of roughly 10 square km, that had no strategic value. The cost was 500,000 killed. The fighting was so intense, and the lines so static, that the dead of 1914 lay beside those of 1918. Battles swept back and forth churning up the graves of previous battles, and not allowing for the proper burial of the slain. Often the attempt to bury was more dangerous than the battle itself. Burials, if made at all, were more for reasons of hygiene, rather than a point of honour.

The Hill 60-Mount Sorrel-Hill 62-Hooge sector, (and the village of Zillebeke, which was directly behind the lines) was a hotly contested front-line for the entire war. Consequently cemeteries are more numerous around Zillebeke than any other part of the Salient.

After the Battle of Mount Sorrel the Canadian dead lay scattered in the destroyed trenches, and shell holes or among the shattered and burned tree-stumps that once were Sanctuary and Armagh Woods and Maple Copse. Gone too were the battlefield cemeteries from before the battle, smashed by a million shells that had plastered the ground. When the Irish Guards relieved the Canadians after the fighting, their historian, Rudyard Kipling wrote: "their right line for nearly half a mile, was absolutely unrecognizable save in a few isolated spots. The shredded ground was full of buried iron and timber which made digging difficult, and, in spite of a lot of cleaning up by predecessors, dead Canadians lay in every corner. It ran through what had been a wood and was now a dreary collection of charred and splintered stakes, 'to the top of which, blown there by shells, hung tatters of khaki uniform and equipment.' There was no trace of any communication trenches." In addition to the terrible battle field conditions there was no dual identification tag system (it came into effect later in 1916) and many soldiers had no identification on them at all. Others had their personal effects or aluminum ID bracelets removed when buried or taken as souvenirs, so when the battlefields were cleared after the war, no identification remained on the bodies.

Consequently few of the Canadian soldiers slain in the battle have a known grave. Of the estimated 2,600 killed more than 2,000 are commemorated by name only on the Menin Gate Memorial. Those who died of wounds after being evacuated rest in known graves at Ypres, Poperinghe or on the French coast. Only a few hundred of those killed in the fighting rest beneath a named headstone. During the clearing of the Salient in 1919-1921 and the discovery of remains since that time, many more remains were found. Some were identified, but as local cemeteries were full, the remains were taken many miles away from where they had died. Today the Canadians who died in the Battle of Mount Sorrel rest in dozens of cemeteries around Ypres, stretching from Langemarck to Ploegsteert. But most are interred in the beautiful cemeteries that now surround the haunted village of Zillebeke.

There are more than 9,700 First World War Canadian dead buried in 160 cemeteries in Belgium. There are also hundreds of Canadians, killed in the Second World War buried in the main Canadian War Cemeteries in central and eastern Belgium at Adegem and Antwerp.

The Menin Gate Memorial

The Menin Gate Memorial, on the eastern edge of the old town on the Ypres-Menin road, is a Memorial to the Missing or soldiers who died in the Ypres Salient and have no known grave (NKG). It is unique among British Commonwealth memorials to the missing in that the nations of the Commonwealth chose it as the place of commemoration for their men missing in Belgium. Only the New Zealanders have commemorated elsewhere. The names of 55,000 soldiers from Britain (40,244), India (421), Australia (6,198), South Africa (564), Canada (6,983; the graves of 80 have since been identified), and the British West Indies (6), adorn the walls of this impressive memorial. Even today the numbers continue to change as more names are added and some removed as graves are identified. The massive Memorial itself was not large enough to count the sacrifice of the men at Ypres. So enormous were the numbers of missing that a second memorial listing 33,804 names, of British (killed after August 15, 1917) soldiers, 1,179 New Zealanders and one Newfoundlander, had to be built at Tyne Cot.

For Canada the Menin Gate is the point of commemoration for all Canadians missing in Belgium, 1914-1918. (Those Canadian soldiers missing in France are commemorated on the Vimy Memorial, north of Arras.) It is the principal place of commemoration for soldiers who died in the Battle of Mount Sorrel. They represent 23% of the Canadian names on the memorial. The balance of the missing were lost in the battles of Ypres 1915 (roughly 1,200), St. Eloi 1916, and Passchendaele 1917.

The panels are arranged by unit (in order of service and numbered battalion), rank, and alphabetically. Every name has a story.

Near the top of the list for CANADIAN ARTILLERY is Lieutenant Alexis H. Helmer, whose death inspired his friend John McCrae to write the poem "In Flanders Fields".

Amongst the 64 names listed as the Missing from the CANADIAN ENGINEERS panels are 22 members of the No. 2 Tunnelling Company killed in the Battle of Mount Sorrel. Most were trapped when their galleries dug under the German position at "the Birdcage" were collapsed by a camouflet.

The PRINCESS PATRICIA'S C. L. I. panels list the names of 504 missing and reflect the three times the unit was wiped out in the Salient. Topping the panel is Major Talbot Papineau, killed at Passchendaele in 1917. Captain Harry Dennison was killed at Frezenberg on May 8th, 1915. His Brother Ralph was killed the same day serving as a officer in the Royal Sussex Regiment. For those familiar with "Letters of Agar Adamson" the names on the officer's panel reads like an index.

Amongst the senior NCOs is Company Sergeant Major James W. Dames, DCM, whose grave was identified in 1991. This Boer War hero is now known to be buried in Hagle Dump Cemetery, Belgium. Twenty-one year old Frank Smith Brown of Montreal, known as the "Poet of the Pats" is commemorated near the top of the SERGEANT's panel. He was killed February 3rd, 1915

William Dalgleish Ford
Private
Princess Patricia's Canadian L.I.
Killed in action June 2nd, 1916.
Born at Portneuf Station, Quebec,
April 22nd, 1890. Older brother
of Eric Allan Ford.
Enlisted at Montreal in the 2nd
University Coy. and transferred to
the PPCLI in September 1915.
On the afternoon of June 2nd,
1916 he was in the forward
trenches in Sanctuary Wood, with
his brother, when he was killed in
the German trench mortar bombardment at the Loop. His body
was not recovered and he is commemorated by name only on the
Menin Gate Memorial.

Eric Allan Ford
Corporal
Princess Patricia's Canadian L.I.
Killed in action June 2nd, 1916.
Born at Portneuf Station, Quebec,
January 27th, 1892. Son of
Joseph and Mary Jessica Ford of
Portneuf.
Enlisted in the 5th CMR in 1915
and transferred to the PPCLI in
April 1916.
On the afternoon of June 2nd,
1916 he was with his men in the
advanced positions in Sanctuary
Wood, when he was killed in the
inundation of German trench
mortar fire that hit the posts at
the Loop. He has no known grave
and is commemorated on the
Menin Gate Memorial.

near St.Eloi. A book of his poems "Contingent Ditties" was published shortly after his death.

Under LANCE CORPORAL is William D. Ford who was killed June 2nd, 1916 in Sanctuary Wood. His brother Eric was killed the same day, and can be found under PRIVATE. Just two names down are brothers Hubert and Leonard Foster of London, England. They were both killed by the same shell, June 30th, 1916. This incidence of brothers being killed, often on the same day is sadly common. On the PPCLI panels there at least three other sets of brothers listed, and as this memorial only accounts for 10% of those who fell, the losses cannot even be imagined. Knowing the sacrifice of Canadians and all Commonwealth troops at Ypres, is it any wonder this place was held in such reverence by their generation, and why Ypres should always be remembered.

At the top of the 4TH. BN. CANADIAN INFANTRY panel is Lieutenant Colonel Arthur Birchall, the commanding officer, killed near Turco Farm on Mauser Ridge in April 1915. Killed with Birchall was Captain John Glover. Glover's brother Sergeant Norman Glover was killed the same day serving with the 10th Battalion at Kitchener's Wood.

Private James Henderson of Vancouver, serving with the 7th Battalion was only 24 when killed at Ypres in 1915. Whether it was for vengeance, or a sense of duty, his father, Peter, enlisted and served with the 103rd Battalion. He also died on active service.

On the panels of the 8TH. BN. CANADIAN INFANTRY is Company Sergeant Major Frederick W. Hall, VC, who died helping wounded comrades near Gravenstafel Ridge in 1915. He was killed by a sniper. But his courage so impressed his superiors, he was awarded the Victoria Cross, posthumously. Private Daniel Robertson was killed proceeding the recapture of Mount Sorrel when the Germans continually strafed the hill. His father, Daniel Sr., served with the 87th Battalion. He too was killed in action during the Battle of the Somme, November 18th, 1916. Amongst the Privates listed is Charles D. Middleton, killed also on June 14th. He was one of six brothers who served, five with the Canadians. Archibald died of wounds in October 1916, John was killed at Vimy, and his brother-in-law was killed in 1918. The others survived.

At the top of the 10TH. BN. CANADIAN INFANTRY panel is the name of Captain Charles T. Costigan, DSO, MC. Costigan was an original member of the Battalion and was killed at Passchendaele in November 1917. In 1992 a grave in Passchendaele New British Cemetery was positively identified as Costigan's. A new headstone was erected and his place of commemoration is now in the cemetery. Listed under PRIVATE are James and William Farquhar, both killed June 3rd, 1916 in the failed counter-attack on Observatory Ridge. They were 38 and 34 years old respectively. A few names away is Harold Goodall from Surrey, England, who was killed April 22nd, 1915 at Kitchener's Wood. Ernest, his older brother by 10 years, was killed 10 days later, and is listed with the 3rd Bn. Canadian Infantry.

On the 13TH. BN. CANADIAN INFANTRY panel is Lance Corporal Frederick Fisher, VC, who died valiantly covering the open flank just north of the Ypres-Poelcapelle road and west of Poelcapelle on April 23rd, 1915. SERGEANT Donald Salmon was killed at Passchendaele in November 1917. He was one of seven brothers from Norwich, England who served in the war.

Two hundred and fifty names of missing 15th BN. CANADIAN INFANTRY fill six panels, and amongst them is Lance Corporal Frank Tarr of West Monckton, Ontario, killed November 1917. His brother Private Henry Tarr (on the 2nd Bn. Canadian Infantry panels) was killed July 25th, 1916 at the Bluff. Private John Forbes Philip from Aberdeen, Scotland was killed at Ypres in 1915. During the war his father and five brothers fought in the war. Two of them were killed. Lance Corporal Burton M. West was killed June 3rd, 1916. His brother Gordon B. West, killed February 5th, 1916, is listed under CORPORAL on the 10th Bn. Canadian Infantry panels.

In reading the Commonwealth War Graves Registers for the Menin Gate Memorial (there are 37 Parts, with five containing only Canadian entries), one of the most shocking sights reveals the sad story of the three Aitkens brothers of Winnipeg, Manitoba. Privates George and James were killed with the 16th

Battalion on April 23rd, 1915 and their brother John, was killed one year later, April 6th, 1916 at St. Eloi (27th Bn. Canadian Infantry). It is not known if other brothers served or survived.

Under SERGEANT on the 16TH BN. CANADIAN INFANTRY panels is Norman J. McKenzie from Sault Ste.Marie, Ontario, who was killed April 23rd, 1915 at Kitchener's Wood. His brother, Lieutenant Wallace A. McKenzie was killed two days later, and is listed on the 8th Bn. Canadian Infantry panel.

One of the great memoirs of the Great War was written by Will R. Bird who served with the 42nd Battalion from late 1916 to the end of the war. "Ghosts Have Warm Hands" (or "And We Go On" in its 1930 incarnation) told of Bird's trench experiences with vivid accuracy, but devoid of sentimentality. Two of its strongest episodes occur when Will's younger brother, Stephen, a Corporal in the 25th Canadian Infantry from Nova Scotia, visits him just in time to save his life. Will's good fortune seems divine and when you realize Stephen was killed in a mine explosion on the Kemmel front in October 1915, the story takes on a ghostly air. That in conjunction with Bird's hard, factual style sends chills down your spine. Stephen Bird is the third name down under PRIVATE on the 25TH. BN. CANADIAN INFANTRY panel.

On the 28TH. BN. CANADIAN INFANTRY panel there are 260 names, by far the most of any Second Division unit. Most of the men were killed at St. Eloi Craters, Passchendaele or at Hooge, when the mines were blown under their positions on June 6th, 1916. There are two sets of brothers listed under PRIVATE. Reuben and William Gillespie of Mawer, Saskatchewan and Allen and John Woodside of Port Arthur, Ontario, were all killed at Hooge on June 6th.

Private Francis Savoie of the 42ND. BN. CANADIAN INFANTRY, was only 16 years old when he was killed in the counter-attack on Sanctuary Wood, June 3rd, 1916. He enlisted when he was only 15!

The 49TH BN. CANADIAN INFANTRY, from Alberta fought their first major battle at Mount Sorrel. Among the fallen was Sergeant Harold T. Morgan killed June 2nd, 1916 trying to recapture Sanctuary Wood. His brother Herbert was killed the same day in the Wood (see PRIVATE, PPCLI). They were from

Guildford, England. Listed amongst the Privates is William C. Sample of Blenheim, Ontario, killed at Passchendaele, October 30th, 1917 when the unit suffered 443 casualties fighting up Bellevue spur. Harry, his brother was killed four days earlier on the Passchendaele Ridge (see panels 50th Bn. Canadian Infantry).

Further down the PRIVATE list is Harold E. White of Orangeville, Ontario. He was killed in a German trench raid in Sanctuary Wood, May 1st, 1916. His brother, Howard A. White, was killed serving with the Royal Canadian Regiment at Lens in August 1917, and is commemorated on the Vimy Memorial. They were the sons of William and Margaret White. Margaret never stopped grieving the loss of her two boys. She was known to pray and cry for them every night. On every Remembrance Day for 25 years she laid the wreath at the Cenotaph in Toronto, representing Orangeville.

The highest ranking officer listed on the 52ND BN. CANADIAN INFANTRY panel is Lieutenant Colonel Archibald E. Hay, 42 years-old, from Quebec City. He was killed during the Third Division's counter-attack on Sanctuary Wood, June 3rd, 1916.

The longest list of missing belongs to the CANADIAN MOUNTED RIFLES. There are 721 of them belonging to the four CMR Battalions (1st, 2nd, 4th and 5th) that made up the 8th Canadian Infantry Brigade of the Third Division. They suffered enormous casualties at Mount Sorrel and Hill 62, and the highest ranking officer listed is Lieutenant-Colonel Alfred Ernest Shaw. He was killed June 3rd (probably the 2nd), 1916. Private Harold E. Benjamin of the 5th CMR was killed at Maple Copse, June 2nd, 1916. His brother Sergeant Percy was killed at Passchendaele in October, 1917. They were the sons of J.N. Benjamin of Pugwash, Nova Scotia. Private Walter G. Forbes was killed June 2nd, 1916 at Mount Sorrel (4th CMR). His two brothers Joseph and Gilbert were also killed in the war.

The CANADIAN MACHINE GUN CORPS panels list 161 names. Under LIEUTENANT is Hugh McKenzie, DCM, killed attacking a German pillbox on the Bellevue spur, October 30th, 1917. McKenzie won the Victoria Cross, posthumously, for his bravery that day. "V.C." is engraved in front of his name. (Interestingly U.S. Memorials to the Missing engrave a symbol of the Decoration in front of the late soldier's name.)

Many Nations were represented in the Canadian Corps of 1914-1918. Examining the Canadian Registers for the Menin Gate Memorial the home addresses seem to come from every Country; England, Ireland, Scotland, the United States, Jamaica, Italy, Holland, Denmark, Finland, Yugoslavia, Mexico, Sweden, France, Montenegro, and even Germany (Private F. Bob, PPCLI), to mention a few. But there are also Belgians. Private William Vangheluwe served with the CMGC, and was killed at Passchendaele, October 29th, 1917. He died 20 km from his home in Batatia, Roulers. Another Belgian, also killed at Passchendaele, Private Theophildus Van Vaerenburgh of the 102nd Bn. Canadian Infantry. He was a native of Nieuwerkerken, Aalst. Not on the Memorial, but buried in Antwerpen (Kiel) Cemetery is the most unusual burial of a Belgian serving Canada. Private Jurien Cuperus, CASC, died in Canada in December 1916. After the war his body was brought back and buried in Belgian soil.

The final name on the Canadian panels belongs to Captain (Honourary) DeWitt Bolton Irwin, CANADIAN Y.M.C.A., of Collingwood, Ontario. He was killed in the fighting for Kitchener's Wood on April 23rd, 1915.

Designed by Sir Reginald Bloomfield, the memorial was unveiled in 1927. Every night at 8 p.m., traffic on both sides of the memorial comes to a halt while buglers of the Ypres Fire Brigade sound The Last Post. This is a very moving experience.

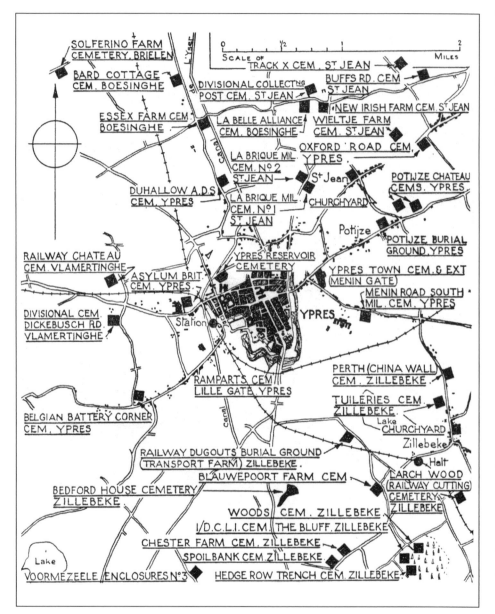

Map of the Cemeteries around Ypres.

The Cemeteries where most of the soldiers killed in the Battle of Mount Sorrel rest are located near the village of Zillebeke. These cemeteries are usually large and contain a mixture of original burials and concentrations.

Railway Dugouts (Transport Farm) Burial Ground, Zillebeke

The cemetery is three km south of Ypres. Exit Ypres through the Lille Gate at Shrapnel Corner turn left to Zillebeke, after one km the cemetery appears on the right.

The cemetery was made by fighting units starting in April 1915 and was used to the end of the war. It was enlarged by the concentration of 422 remains in 1924. It now contains 2,460 Commonwealth graves or special commemorations. There are 636 Canadian burials* including 85 unknowns. The majority were killed holding the line near Zillebeke in 1916.

The cemetery is characteristic of many in the Salient. The original graves are often in no specific order, and reflect the losses of a particular unit after a particular tour. A section would then be used to accommodate some of the thousands of remains found between 1919 and the 1930s. Also characteristically, is a plot or row commemorating the graves from another cemetery, that were registered and later destroyed in battle, lost or "Believed" or "Known" "to be buried in this cemetery". These are called "Special Memorials" or "Kipling's", as the headstones usually have Kipling's phrase "Their Glory Shall Not Be Blotted Out" engraved at the base. Often the headstones are centred by a large block of Portland Stone, called a "Duhallow Block". They are normally located along the walls of the cemetery so as not to confuse a Special Memorial with a real burial. Railway Dugouts has a large grouping of 259 Special Memorials. They are located inside the entrance. Seventy-three Canadians buried in Valley Cottages Cemetery (on Observatory Ridge) whose graves were destroyed are commemorated here. Two of the Special Memorials belong to the Wild brothers, Frederick and Reginald,

Note: The figures for burials represent men, known or unknown, buried in a cemetery, and soldiers specially commemorated there, whose remains are not actually in the cemetery.

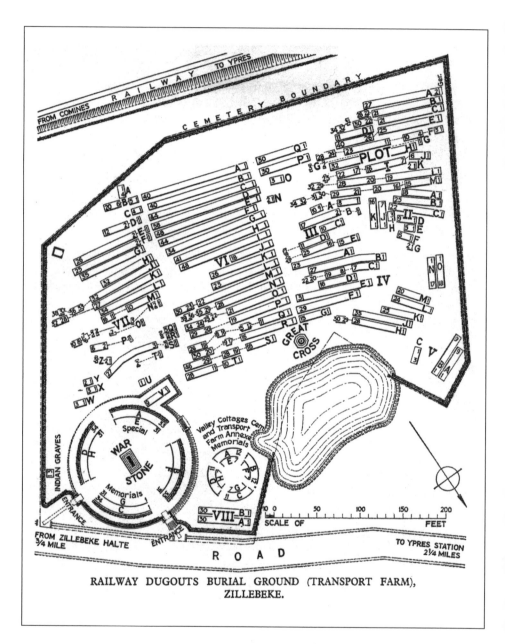

RAILWAY DUGOUTS BURIAL GROUND (TRANSPORT FARM),
ZILLEBEKE.

Ypres Railway Dugouts, April-May 1919.
(PUBLIC ARCHIVES OF CANADA PA 4594)

of Islington, Ontario. They were both killed August 21st, 1916.

Amongst the original burials is the grave (Plot VI, Row D, Grave 32) of Private Henry Pope of the 16th (Canadian Scottish) Battalion killed June 4th, 1916. Henry was one of three brothers from Quebec City killed in the war. Charles was killed May 7th, 1916 and is commemorated by Special Memorial in Maple Copse Cemetery. He was a Lieutenant in the PPCLI. The third brother, Private Ernest was killed at Passchendaele on November 10th, 1917 and is commemorated on the 7th Bn. Canadian Infantry panels on the Menin Gate.

The concentrations brought in many Canadians from the Mount Sorrel area, and 40 others from the battlefield of the Second Battle of Ypres. The great majority are unidentified.

There is one Victoria Cross winner buried in Plot I, Row O, Grave 3. Lieutenant Frederick Youens of the Durham Light Infantry won his VC near Hill 60, July 7th, 1917. He was mortally wounded in the action and died on July 9th.

Brigade H.Q. in Bedford House Grounds, April-May 1919.

Bedford House Cemetery, Zillebeke

Bedford House Cemetery is located 2 km south of Ypres on the east side of the road to Lille (Rijsel). It is an enormous cemetery consisting of four enclosures over an area of 4.6 hectares. The landscaping of this cemetery is beautiful, complete with moats, iron bridges and the ruins of the old Rosendal Chateau. (Also known as "Bedford House" or "Woodcote House".)

The chateau grounds were used as headquarters for many units, and field ambulances. Cemeteries were made to bury the dead. Gradually Bedford House came to hold five Enclosures. Enclosures No. 1 and No. 5 were concentrated to other Cemeteries elsewhere in the Salient. Enclosures No. 2 and No. 4 were greatly expanded in the post-war period by the concentrations from the surrounding battlefields and smaller cemeteries. Enclosure No. 3 was left "as is".

Enclosure No. 2

This Enclosure was started by fighting units in December 1915 and used to the end of the war. After the war two large cemeteries from Ypres were concentrated here. The cemeteries: Ecole de Bienfaisance and Asylum British, held 437 graves.

The Enclosure now contains 695 Commonwealth war dead, including 21 Canadians, (all identified). None of the burials are associated with Mount Sorrel.

Enclosure No. 3

This is the smallest of the Enclosures and contains 60 known graves including 5 Canadians. It is approached by an iron bridge from Enclosure No. 4. It is a very pretty area and historically significant in that it shows exactly how front line burials were made.

Enclosure No. 4

This is the largest Enclosure and is located at the eastern part of the cemetery. Originally it contained a small number of burials (Plot I and II), but was expanded in 1921-23 by the concentration of 3,324 graves from the surrounding area. It now contains 3,860 Commonwealth graves (2,478 are unknowns) or commemorations that include 309 Canadians, of whom 130 are unidentified. One hundred and twenty-five burials are associated with the Battle of Mount Sorrel, the majority are spread throughout the cemetery, although Plot I contains a number of 2nd Division men killed in the battle. Two brothers, George and Sydney Hamilton of the 21st (Eastern Ontario) Battalion, both killed June 14th, 1916, are buried in Plot I, Row P, Grave 3 and Row K, Grave 22 respectively.

There is one Victoria Cross winner in the cemetery. Second Lieutenant Rupert Hallowes, Middlesex Regiment, won his V.C. posthumously in the vicious fighting at Hooge at the end of September 1915. He is buried in Plot XIV, Row B, Grave 36.

Enclosure No. 6

Enclosure No. 6 is unique in that it contains burials of those whose remains were found in the Salient between 1937 and 1939. It is the first Enclosure on your left as you approach the entrance and is entered by crossing an iron bridge.

The Enclosure contains 534 burials of which 499 are unidentified. There are 13 identified Canadian graves here and 42 unidentified. Thirty-seven of the graves were found in a variety of locations on the Mount Sorrel battlefield.

Perth (China Wall) Cemetery, Zillebeke

Perth Cemetery is 4 km east of Ypres on the road to Zillebeke. It is located on the north side of the village.

It was started by the French in 1914 and used by British units until October 1917, at which time it contained 130 graves (Plot I). From 1919 to 1924 more than 2,500 graves were brought in, including many from the Battlefields of the Second Battle of Ypres, 1915.

The cemetery now contains 2,763 Commonwealth burials of which 1,368 are unidentified. There are 133 Canadians, including 77 unknowns, buried here. The majority of the Canadians were killed in April 1915 but 36 (mostly unknown) are associated with Mount Sorrel.

Two Victoria Cross winners are buried here. Major W.H. Johnston, VC, Royal Engineers, (Plot III, Row C, Grave 12) won a famous VC for transporting wounded and munitions back-and-forth across the Aisne river, under heavy fire in September 1914. He was killed June 8th, 1915 near Ypres.

Second Lieutenant Frederick Birks, VC, MM, 6th Australian Infantry, won his VC, posthumously, at Glencourse Wood, September 1917 in the Battle of Passchendaele. He is buried in Plot I, Row G, Grave 45.

Zillebeke Churchyard

The village of Zillebeke was destroyed during the war. The cemetery is located beside the church in the village. Although there are only a few Canadians buried in it, it is interesting to reflect on the importance of the village, a heroic place during the Great War.

The Churchyard contains 32 original burials, including 14 blue-blooded officers of the British regular Army killed in the First Battle of Ypres in 1914. Dying that early in the war they seem almost like forgotten men.

The Register of burials reads like a British Who's Who. Names like Rt. Hon. Congleton, de Gunzburg (son of Baroness de Gunzburg), Lord Gordon Lennox, Lieutenant Colonel Scott (son of Major General Scott), and Symes-Thompson,. The Regiments represent all that is Royal: Grenadier Guards, Coldstream Guard, 13th Hussars, Life Guards and Royal Horse Guards. They are like something from another era, an era that ended at Ypres.

There are ten Canadians buried here, four are unidentified. They received a quick burial in the churchyard during the Battle of Mount Sorrel. A platoon of the 24th (Queen Victoria's Rifles) Battalion was marching through Zillebeke on the night of June 6th/7th, 1916. A large German shell made a direct hit in the group as they passed single file by the church. Their history reported, "Twelve men lay dead on the road... and eleven severely wounded lay amongst them. Arms and legs were strewn around and in the darkness the nightmare was to separate the wounded and dying from the dead... the dead were carried to the roadside to await the completion of arrangements for their burials..."

Two identified members of No. 5 platoon are interred here: Privates Croft and Sime (they are also commemorated on the Menin Gate). Three others rest in unidentified graves.

From the back of the cemetery Maple Copse and Sanctuary Wood Cemetery (and the museum) can be seen.

Larch Wood (Railway Cutting) Cemetery, Zillebeke

The Cemetery is located 1 km south-west of Zillebeke village, about 1 km up an access road, on the north-east side of the railway line.

It was started by fighting units in April 1915 and used until 1918, when it contained 600 graves. After the war 245 graves were brought in from the surrounding battlefields and Commonwealth graves from 18 German cemeteries, where they died as POWs.

It now contains 856 Commonwealth graves including 86 Canadians (10 are unidentified). The majority of the graves belong to the 5th (Saskatchewan) Battalion, 35 graves, and the 16th (Canadian Scottish) Battalion, also 35 graves.

Thirty-two of the 5th Battalion men were killed on Hill 60 between June 2nd and 6th. They are buried in Plot IV and V.

An unusual Canadian burial is found in Plot IV, Row F, Grave 9. Chief Officer E. Woods of the Merchant Marines was serving on the S.S. "Mascota" and died as a POW at Bruges General Cemetery March 30th, 1917.

Maple Copse Cemetery, Zillebeke

The Cemetery is located one km east of Zillebeke village in a small wood known as Maple Copse. The Cemetery was used by fighting units and most of the burials were made in the spring of 1916. During the heavy fighting in June 1916 (where the 5th CMR made their stand) the cemetery was obliterated. After the war the locations of the graves could not be identified so Special Memorials were erected to commemorate those known to be buried there. The result is quite a unique design. Only 26 identified graves are marked. The 230 remaining known burials are commemorated by headstones superscribed "Known to be buried in this cemetery".

Three hundred and eight Commonwealth soldiers are commemorated here, including 154 Canadians (including 12 unidentified). This beautiful cemetery (surrounded by a moat) contains the graves of only a handful of Mount Sorrel casualties. Lieutenant Charles Pope, PPCLI, killed June 2nd, 1916, one of three brothers killed in the war (see Railway Dugouts Burial Ground) and Private Raymond Burton of the Eaton's Motor Machine Gun Battery, killed June 13th, are commemorated here. The Eaton's MMGB was privately financed by Timothy Eaton, founder of the Eaton's Department Store and Catalogue chain.

Also buried in Maple Copse is Captain the Honourable, Alfred Shaughnessy of Montreal and son of the President of the Canadian Pacific Railway. He was killed March 31st, 1916 and left a widow and three small children.*

Among the Special Memorials are 22 erected to Canadian infantry attached to the No. 2 Tunnelling Company, Canadian

* see "Tapestry of War" by S. Gwyn. Harper Collins, 1992.

Engineers. In February 1917 they were suffocated by smoke from a fire which broke out in the underground gallery they were working in. It is unlikely they are actually buried here.

Hooge Crater Cemetery, Zillebeke

Hooge is a hamlet , located four km south-east of Ypres on a high point on the road to Menin. Hooge was the scene of fierce fighting throughout the war and the hamlet changed hands several times. Mining warfare was used extensively here and the whole area became a quagmire of craters. The cemetery is located on the south side of the road. It was originally only 76 graves but was greatly expanded after the war by the concentration of 5,800 graves from the battlefields and smaller cemeteries. It now contains 5,892 burials in commemorations including 105 Canadians (36 are unidentified).

Twenty-five of those buried here were killed in the Battle of Mount Sorrel. Their bodies were found in 1919. During those clearances the Exhumation Company found a cross to Private Westover, 1st (Western Ontario) Canadian Infantry. As they dug

View of Hooge and Hooge Crater Cemetery.

(N. CHRISTIE)

they found more and more bodies until 20 bodies were recovered. They were all 1st Battalion, all killed July 9th, 1916 when the Germans blew mines in Sanctuary Wood. Amongst those found were the remains of Private Eugene Flagg. A few months later they were digging in a shell hole in Sanctuary Wood and found more than 30 bodies and amongst them was Private Ronald Flagg, the brother of Eugene Flagg. He had been killed April 26th, 1916. They were the sons of George and Annie Flagg of Grand Manan, New Brunswick. They are buried in Plot XVII, Row E, grave 16 and Plot XVI, Row F, Grave 1, respectively.

Probably the last Canadian to be killed in the Salient, Sapper Henry Nores, 10th Battalion, Canadian Railway Troops, killed in action October 15th, 1918, is buried in Plot XIX, Row J, Grave 3.

One Victoria cross winner is buried in Hooge Crater. Private Patrick Bugden of the 31st Battalion, A.I.F., is buried in Plot VIII, Row C, Grave 5. He won the Victoria Cross, posthumously for bravery at Polygon Wood, September 28th, 1917.

Sanctuary Wood Cemetery, Zillebeke

Sanctuary Wood Cemetery is located 4 km south-east of Ypres. It is located on the road leading from the Menin road, south to the Hill 62 Canadian Battlefield Memorial. It can be seen from Maple Copse and Hooge Crater Cemeteries.

The cemetery was one of three established in Sanctuary Wood in the summer of 1915. It was badly destroyed in the Battle of Mount Sorrel. At the end of the war it contained 137 graves (Plot I) but was greatly enlarged by the concentration of isolated graves and small cemeteries over the period, 1927 to 1932. The triangle-shaped cemetery now contains 1,989 Commonwealth burials or commemorations including 144 Canadians (71 are unidentified).

Many of the headstones are superscribed "Buried near this spot". "Buried near this spot" does not mean buried near this spot. It is used when a group of graves were found and identified, but not individually, but as a group. Upon exhumation it was not possible to identify who was who. So headstones would be erected, in alphabetical order, over the burials. Consequently every man received a headstone, but the headstone would not be marking the actual grave. This is the defined condition for using the collective term, "Buried near this spot".

From the back of the cemetery there is an excellent view of Maple Copse and the Mount Sorrel battlefield.

Roughly half of the Canadians buried here were killed in the Battle of Mount Sorrel, but unfortunately most are not identified.

Company Sergeant-Major Dudley G. Wright of the 58th (Central Ontario) Canadian Infantry is buried in Plot III, Row B, Grave 25. He was killed in the recapture of Hill 62, June 13th, 1916. In 1927 an Exhumation Company found an unknown CSM - 58th Canadian Infantry and reburied him in Plot III. In a review of CWGC documents it was discovered only one CSM was unaccounted for. Consequently a new headstone bearing the name of CSM D.G. Wright was erected over his long, unidentified grave.

In the Zillebeke area there are several other cemeteries that contain some Canadians killed at Mount Sorrel, although the majority of the graves are associated with other battles. Two km south of the old southern sector of the Salient are five cemeteries: Woods, 1/D.C.L.I., Hedge Row, Chester Farm and Spoilbank. (Only Woods Cemetery has relevance to the Battle of Mount Sorrel.) They contain the many dead - the trench wastage - from holding the line at "The Bluff", one of the most feared places in the Salient. On a nice day it is peaceful to walk along the old farm roads and into the fields of blowing wheat, to visit them. It is hard to believe such horrors took place here. Should you follow my advice be sure to follow the trail into the Palingbeek Provincial Domain, a pretty route through the area of the old Comines Canal. Though tranquil there is much evidence of the war in the undergrowth.

Woods Cemetery, Zillebeke

The cemetery is located six km south of Ypres on the road to Lille (Rijsel), and two km south of Zillebeke. It is located in a farmer's field 800 metres south of the Lille road.

This oddly-shaped cemetery contains only original burials and illustrates how frontline regiments buried their dead.

The cemetery was used by fighting units from 1915 to 1917

and contains 326 Commonwealth graves including 111 Canadians (all identified). Only a few of those buried here were killed at Hill 60 (8th Canadian Infantry) in early June 1916. Most of the Canadians are men from the 1st Division killed April to July 1916. Typical of a frontline - trench wastage - cemetery, there are few officers buried here.

Menin Road Cemetery, Ypres

Menin Road Cemetery is located two km south-east of Ypres, on the south side of the Menin Road. It was used by fighting units from January 1916 to mid-1918.

After the war 203 graves were brought into it from the surrounding battlefields. It now contains 1,634 Commonwealth graves, including 148 Canadians (2 are unidentified).

The majority of the Canadians buried here are 3rd Division men, killed between March and August 1916. Seventeen of the graves belong to men killed in the Battle of Mount Sorrel, including many of the Royal Canadian Regiment killed at Hooge.

Menin Road South Mititary Cemetery, Ypres. c. 1928
(Notice the light gauge railway.)

Ypres Reservoir Cemetery, c. 1928

Ypres Reservoir Cemetery

The cemetery is an easy walk north-west from the Grote Markt in the centre of Ypres. The cemetery, north of the prison (as it was known) was one of three cemeteries located near the Western Gate of the town. It was used continuously throughout the war and contained 1,099 graves (now Plot I). After the war it was enlarged by the battlefield clearances and the concentration of several smaller cemeteries. It now contains 2,611 Commonwealth graves, including 151 Canadians (48 are unknown). More than a third of the Canadian soldiers buried here were killed in the Battle of Mount Sorrel, and these remains were brought into the cemetery during the clearances, 1919-1923. Most are unidentified.

Of interest are the graves in Plot I, Row H which contain the remains of twenty men of the 123rd Canadian Pioneer Battalion killed by one shell on October 21st, 1917. Private W. Tobias of the 123rd, was an Indian Chief from the Brantford Reserve.

Buried in Grave 76 in that row is Private Thomas Moles of the 54th (British Columbia) Canadian Infantry. Moles was executed for desertion and one of 25 Canadians executed in the Great War.*

The cemetery contains a large number of high-ranking British Officers, several Lieutenant-Colonels, and two Generals. The Generals are: Brigadier-General Arthur Lowe, CMG, DSO, killed in action November 24th, 1917, and Brigadier General Francis (Frank) Maxwell, VC, DSO, commanding officer of the 27th Brigade of the 9th (Scottish) Division. Maxwell was killed by a sniper on September 21st, 1917. His Victoria Cross was awarded for bravery during the Boer War, 1899-1902. He is buried in Plot I, Row A, Grave 37.

Brandhoek Military Cemetery, Vlamertinghe

Brandhoek Military Cemetery is located on the south side of the road to Poperinghe, four km west of Ypres. There are three "Brandhoek" cemeteries, and five other cemeteries along this route. During the war Field Ambulances and Dressing Stations were located here, a secure distance away from German artillery fire. Burials in these cemeteries are usually "died of wounds" or artillerymen, unlucky enough to be located by their German counterparts. The Military Cemetery was used from May 1915 until July 1917. It contains the bodies of 665 Commonwealth dead, including 63 Canadians. Fourteen of these men were killed or died of wounds received at the Battle of Mount Sorrel.

Amongst those buried here are: Brigidier F.J. Heyworth, C.B., DSO, killed in action May 9th, 1916 (II.C.2.), and Captain Edward Wickson, Royal Flying Corps, of Toronto, who was killed when his Observation Balloon was shot down June 16th, 1917 (I.L.2.).

War was never far away when you were stationed in the Salient, or coming to or going from it for that matter. On the night of August 19th/20th, 1916 the men of the 8th Canadian

* see "For Freedom And Honour?" by A.B. Godefroy. CEF Books, 1998.

Field Ambulance were having a quiet night at Vlamertinghe Mill. "As the 73rd Canadian Battalion was returning from forward positions and had reached Vlamertinghe road just outside the main dressing station at the old mill, one shell landed right in the midst causing much damage..... The war gave many lessons in contrasts, and this was one of them. Imagine if you can a silence, almost death-like, in a concrete room of an old mill, the faint lights showing up sitting figures of men-soldiers waiting and watching during the hours of the night for anything that might happen-possibly enjoying friendly games of cards to while away the hours.... But suddenly all this is changed by just one explosion outside the mill, one shell dropped in the right place, in the midst of marching troops of this new battalion. Their men had just been forward, for instructional purposes only, and were coming back, free from casualties, when the unexpected happened, and the inside of the mill was immediately changed from an almost quiet peacefulness to a scene of extreme activity, with stretcher bearers and ambulances drivers all on the alert, as they brought in the many wounded by the incident, several who died in the dressing station....under these conditions men soon get into the habit of just living practically from hour-to-hour, the future being wrapped in the uncertainty of the fortunes of war."

My grandfather, Private Randall Christie, was one of the ambulance drivers waiting in the mill. The dead of the 73rd Canadians are buried in Plot II.

There are two other cemeteries at Brandhoek. Buried in the New Military Cemetery, 250 metres west, is Captain Noel Chavasse, VC and bar, MC. Chavasse was one of only three men to win the Victoria Cross twice. His second award was posthumous. Captain Chavasse is buried in Plot III, Row B, Grave 15.

Reninghelst New Military Cemetery

Reninghelst is a village 10 km south-west of Ypres. It was behind the Allied lines for the entire war and was a centre of activity for the 2nd Canadian Division from late 1915 until August 1916.

The cemetery contains 791 Commonwealth burials, including 230 Canadians (one is unidentified). It was used by fighting units throughout the war, and there are a number of Canadian Tunnellers buried here. About 30 men are those killed in the Battle of Mount Sorrel. All are 2nd Division.

Amongst those buried here are: Brigadier-General C.W.E. Gordon, commanding the 123rd Infantry Brigade, killed in action July 23rd, 1917 (III. D. 16.), Major William Y. Hunter, Canadian Infantry, seconded to the War Office, killed in action September 28th, 1918 (V. A. 10.).

Like so many cemeteries in the Salient, Reninghelst also contains a family tragedy. Buried in Plot I, Row A, Grave 16, is Lieutenant Charles Godwin, Canadian Field Artillery, who was killed in action April 4th, 1916. Buried in Plot I, Row E, Grave 14 is his brother John, also in the Artillery, who was killed in action July 8th, 1916. They were the sons of Frederick and Anna Godwin of Ottawa, Ontario.

Dickebusch New Military Cemetery

Dickebusch is a village 5 km south-west of Ypres. It was behind the lines for the entire war and was a centre of operations for the 2nd Canadian Division in the spring-summer 1916. The cemetery was used from early 1915 until May 1917 by artillery and fighting units, and field ambulances. It contains 623 Commonwealth graves, including 84 Canadians (all are identified).

Buried in Row J, Graves 28 and 29 are Horace and Cyril Hill, 24th (Queen Victoria's Rifles) Canadian Infantry. They were killed by the same shell explosion April 30th, 1916. Cyril was 19 and Horace was 22 years old. Both were Buglers, and sons of Thomas and Hannah Hill of Montreal, Quebec.

There are ten men buried here that died in the Battle of Mount Sorrel.

Lijssenthoek Military Cemetery, Poperinghe

The second largest Commonwealth War Cemetery in Belgium is two km south-west of Poperinghe (which is 10 km west of Ypres) in open country, amongst the hanging hops, near the small hamlet of Lijssenthoek. This area was the main transportation and communication link with Ypres throughout the war. Heavy and light gauge railways were built to link Poperinghe and Ypres to the supply depots near the Channel coast. It was here that the transfer of supplies, munitions, and reinforcements to the front took place. The return journeys would be used evacuate the wounded. As Lijssenthoek was near the railway siding, at Remy, the wounded were brought to the Casualty Clearing Stations there from the Salient throughout the war.

Typical of a hospital centre cemetery, the men are buried in chronological order and virtually all are identified. The officers have been buried in their own plots. Lijssenthoek is a spectacular cemetery, and historically captures the enormous sacrifices made by the Commonwealth soldiers to hold the Salient. It contains 9,829 Commonwealth burials, of which 1,051 are Canadian (all are identified). Roughly 300 died in the Battle of Mount Sorrel.

The Canadians buried here represent minor and major actions in which Canadians participated in the Ypres Salient between 1916 and 1917, particularly Mount Sorrel and Passchendaele. Fatalities from the former are predominantly buried in Plots VI (Officers), VII and VIII.

There are 79 Canadian Officers buried here including three Lieutenant-Colonels: Arthur W. Tanner, 10th Canadian Field Ambulance, died of wounds June 4th, 1916 (VI.A.6.), Frank Creighton, 1st (Western Ontario) Canadian Infantry, died of wounds June 16th, 1916 (VI.A.26.), and W.R. Marshall, 15th (48th Highlanders of Toronto) Battalion, killed in action May 19th, 1916 (V.A.39.). Buried in Plot VI, Row A, Grave 38, is Major-General Malcolm Mercer, CB, commander of the 3rd Canadian Infantry Division. Killed at Mount Sorrel June 2nd/3rd, 1916, Mercer's body was not found until June 23rd due to the chaotic conditions. It had been unearthed from his temporary grave by a shell burst. He was the highest ranking Canadian to die in the war.

The fighting in the Ypres Salient was hard on families in the Ottawa Valley. There are three sets of brothers from small towns in the Valley buried in Lijssenthoek. Lieutenant Charles Cotton, Canadian Field Artillery, was killed June 2nd, 1916, defending

Observatory Ridge, and Captain Ross Cotton was killed June 13th, 1916, serving with the 16th (Western Scottish) Battalion. They were the sons of Major-General W.H. Cotton of Almonte, Ontario. They are buried in Plot IX, Row A, Grave 7, and Plot VI, Row A, Grave 7, respectively.

Lieutenant Howard MacLaurin, like Ross Cotton, served in the 16th (Western Canadian Scottish). In civilian life he was a dentist from Vankleek Hill, Ontario. He was killed in the same action as Ross Cotton, and is buried in Plot VI, Row A, Grave 34. His brother, Douglas, a McGill University graduate, died of wounds received in action with the 16th Battalion, April 5th, 1916. He was 26 years old. (Plot V, Row C, Grave 36A.). They were the sons of J.R. MacLaurin of Vankleek Hill.

The third set of brothers, Albert and Alfred DeLisle were from Quyon, on the Quebec side of the Ottawa River. Albert was with the 21st (Eastern Ontario) Battalion, and died of wounds June 29th, 1916. His brother was with the 102nd (British Columbia) Battalion and died of wounds September 10th, 1916. He was one of the first deaths the battalion suffered in the war. They are buried in Plot VIII, Row B, Grave 27, and Plot IX, Row D, Grave 19A, respectively.

The concept of keeping officer burials from the other ranks by the designation of an Officer's Plot (even brothers are separated) is unique to those Hospital Centre cemeteries, established early in the war. Cemeteries along the Channel Coast, such as Etaples, Wimereux and Boulogne Eastern all have strict rules for burials. Officers and Nursing Sisters in a Plot, Jews, Hindus, Moslems often have separate plots. At Etaples there is even a Plot for blacks, primarily from the British West Indies Regiment, but one Canadian is included. At Boulogne the officers are considered three times more important than the other ranks. Officers are buried one man to a grave, while other ranks are stacked three to a grave!

Harlebeke New British Cemetery

Harlebeke is located 7 km north-east of Courtrai, which is 30 km south-east of Ypres, and well beyond the Ypres Salient. The cemetery is located north-east of the village. It is interesting because it predominantly contains soldiers who died of wounds as prisoners-of-war, or Royal Flying Corps pilots shot down behind the German lines. The cemetery was originally used for battle casualties killed in the Advance to Victory in October 1918. In 1924-1925 the graves of POWs were brought in from more than 40 German cemeteries.

Harlebeke now contains 1,116 Commonwealth War dead including 30 Canadians (one is unidentified). There are several other Canadians who served in the RAF buried here, but they are considered, for CWGC statistical purposes, British.

Sixteen of those buried here died of wounds after being taken prisoner at Mount Sorrel. They are predominantly 1st CMR and 4th CMR. Three members of the 28th (Saskatchewan) Canadian Infantry mortally wounded and captured at Hooge are also interred here.

THE HOSPITAL CENTRES

The following cemeteries are located along the northern coast of France. The location of all the major General and Stationary Hospitals were in this area, facing the English Channel, for easy evacuation of the wounded to England. They contain the graves of thousands of Commonwealth soldiers who died of wounds received in the Great War and are associated with every Canadian battle from 1915 to 1918.

Wimereux Communal Cemetery, France

Wimereux is 7 km north of Boulogne. The cemetery was used from 1915 to 1918 and contains the graves of 2,847 Commonwealth soldiers, of whom 216 are Canadian. The Canadian burials reflect many battles, but particularly Vimy and Passchendaele. At the entrance of the cemetery is a memorial plaque to Lieutenant Colonel John McCrae, Canadian Army Medical Corps, who died on active service (of pneumonia) January 1918. He is most famous for the poem, In Flanders Fields, he wrote at Ypres in 1915. He is buried in Plot IV, Row H, Grave 3.

Due to ground instability, all the First World War headstones are recumbent.

Boulogne Eastern Cemetery, France

Boulogne is 100 km west of Ypres on the English Channel coast. The cemetery is in the city's eastern sector above the harbor on the road to St. Omer. It was used for hospital burials from 1914 to 1918 and contains 5,578 Commonwealth burials, of which 442 are Canadian. The Canadian burials reflect various actions between 1915 and 1918, including Ypres, Mount Sorrel, the Somme, Vimy and Passchendaele.

Of interest is the grave of Captain Frederick W. Campbell of the 1st Canadian Battalion (Western Ontario). Campbell died on June 19th, 1915 of wounds received in the Battle of Festubert on June 15. His Victoria Cross was awarded for conspicuous bravery at Festubert. He is buried in Plot II, Row A, Grave 24.

There is also a very interesting Portugese Plot and Memorial, and many Second World War graves, including a number of Canadian soldiers killed at Dieppe, August 19th, 1942. Their bodies drifted along the Channel coast and washed up on the beaches near Boulogne.

Etaples Military Cemetery, France

Etaples Cemetery is on the coastal road between Boulogne and Le Treport, 3 km north of Etaples. It was used throughout the war and contains 10,729 Commonwealth graves, including 1,123 Canadians. This cemetery reflects the Canadian losses during the major actions of Mount Sorrel, the Somme, Vimy, Passchendaele and the Advance to Victory.

Etaples was the major depot base for the British army on the Western Front and was the location of the infamous Bull Ring and the British mutiny of 1917.

On May 19th, 1918, German Gotha bombers made direct hits on the No. 1 Canadian General hospital, killing 66 people, including three Canadian nursing sisters. The men killed in the attack are buried in Plots 66, 67 and 68. The Nursing Sisters and officers are buried in Plot 28.

"He is not Missing; He is Here"

There are few memorials that symbolize the slaughter of the Great War as powerfully as the Menin Gate Memorial. Standing 80 feet high this imposing structure commemorates the sacrifice of 200,000 British Empire lives in defence of the Ypres Salient, 1914-1918. It is unique as a British Empire Memorial in that all but one of the nations of the Empire are represented on one of the 59 panels, that list more than 55,000 men killed at Ypres, "whom the fortune of war denied the known and honoured burial given to their comrades in death".

Its location as the Eastern Gate of Ypres is itself significant. Through it led to the devastated land that was known as 'the Salient'. It was certainly "the Gate of Death". Death permeated Ypres during the Great War and standing in the Gate, observing the hundreds of names of the men who marched through that same place 80 years ago sends chills down your spine. You can almost hear the tramping of the hob-nail boots as the soldiers moved quietly through, hidden in darkness of the night.

The location was originally to be the place to commemorate Canada's Fallen, but certainly the need to honour all the Empire's dead was of paramount importance. The Commonwealth (then Imperial) War Graves Commission commissioned one of their principal architects, Sir Reginald Bloomfield to design a monument to the everlasting memory of "the Salient".

His tribute was a structure 135 ft., 6 ins. long, 104 ft wide, and 80 ft high. It had two arches, each surmounted by a Sarcophagus, with the sculpture of a passive lion resting on each sarcophagus. The inner walls were 30 ft. high and on those walls the panels bearing the thousands of names of the missing would bear testament to the sacrifice. It was to be the "Guardian of the Salient", and that it certainly is.

Construction on the gate started in 1923 amidst the ruins of the ancient Flemish city. The entire town was being rebuilt on its old foundations, the rubble was removed and a rebirth was in process.

Five hundred piles were driven 40 ft. deep to ensure a stable foundation. Thousands of unexploded shells were painstakingly

Unveiling of the Menin Gate Memorial.

removed. The skeletons of 28 Belgian civilians killed by German shelling were exhumed. By 1927 the memorial was complete. Six thousand tons of stone, 11,000 tons of concrete and 500 tons of steel were used in the final product. When the weight of the panels and sculptures (by Mr William R. Dick) were added, the Menin Gate Memorial weighed 20,000 tons.

On a beautiful summer's day, Sunday, July 24th, 1927, at 10:30 am, in the presence of thousands of Pilgrims, the long-awaited unveiling of the "Guardian of the Salient" took place. In the presence of Albert, King of the Belgians, many dignitaries, bands and Guards of Honour, Field Marshall Lord Plumer, former commander of the British Second Army, unveiled the Menin Gate Memorial.

Lord Plumer gave a moving speech directed at the families of the missing, who for many years had hoped the bodies of their loved ones would be found. But as Plumer so eloquently stated "there should be erected a memorial worthy of them which should give expression to the nations' gratitude for their sacrifice and their sympathy with those who mourned them. A memorial has been erected which, in its simple grandeur, fulfills this object, and now it can be said of each one in whose honour we are assembled here today; 'He is not missing; he is here'."

Next to speak was King Albert who praised the sacrifice of all soldiers of the British Empire who fell in defence of Belgium. "It is my sense of gratitude which brings me here. I come to render profound and sincere homage in the name of my country to the memory of 90,000 soldiers of the British Empire who died a hero's death for the ideal of justice and liberty. We feel for each and all of them the same sentiments of respect and gratitude...

"It (the memorial) forever consecrates the sublime sacrifice of those gallant soldiers, and will perpetuate their memory for generations to come, but the memory will live also for all time in the hearts of the Belgian people."

With the completion of the Kings' speech, a hymn was sung and prayers were delivered, then buglers sounded the Last Post, and pipers played "the Flower of the Forest" (from atop the ramparts). After the sounds of the Scottish lament faded away there came a minute of silence followed by the crash of bugles playing

"Reveille". Wreaths were laid by many dignitaries at the base of the Arches and the crowd moved in to touch the names on the sacred memorial.

Amongst the many Pilgrims were 700 mothers who lost sons in the war. Many had broken down during the ceremony. Many had waited years to be there. One mother from Toronto, who had lost two sons in the war, said: "I have wanted so much just to see the place where he was laid. These things mean so much to a mother." Another said: "I think he will lie more peacefully now that I have been to see him. He knows that I have been with him today."

More than 70 years later visitors to the Menin Gate do feel closer to those who were there. It still has a ghostly aura and if their spirits are about they are certainly conjured when the Last Post is sounded every night at 8 pm. I swear, you can hear them.

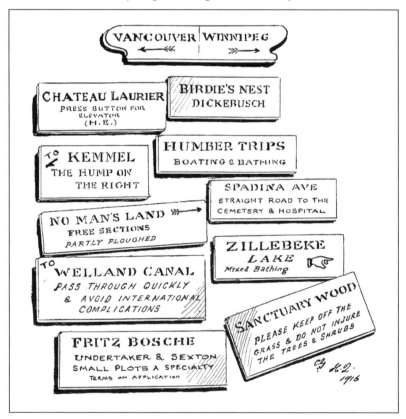

A few Canadian trench signs

The Mystery of Captain Blackader

On the afternoon of June 2nd, 1916 the 42nd (Black Watch of Montreal) Battalion was ordered forward to counter-attack the Germans who had broken through the Canadian lines. At Belgian Chateau, Captain Gordon Blackader, led his men of 'D' Company forward intent on reaching the PPCLI still hanging on in Sanctuary Wood. Shelling was intense and as the Highlanders advanced hot metal shrapnel and shell fragments caused many casualties. Advancing close to Gordon House, at the China Wall, a shell exploded overhead and a splinter struck the Captain in the throat. For him the battle was over and he was quickly evacuated for treatment.

Gordon Home Blackader was born to an affluent family in Montreal, Quebec. Montreal was then the commercial and cultural capital of Canada. Its population was 700,000 people, compared to Toronto's 500,000. Its wealthy families were a tightknit group and Blackader was the cousin of Hamilton Gault of the famous Gault "Cotton King" family. Graduating as an Architect from McGill University Blackader moved successfully into business. Like all upstanding Canadian men he also maintained a commission in one of Montreal's famous Militia units. At the outbreak of war he enlisted with the 42nd Battalion and reached France in September 1915. The Battalion had seen little fighting until that June day and for Captain Blackader his first battle was be his last.

Blackader was removed from the battlefield and sent to England where the Regimental History indicated he died of wounds on August 10th, 1916. It is also at this point that Blackader disappears from the Records. The CWGC had no record of him. He was apparently not buried anywhere nor was he commemorated on a Memorial to the Missing. It was (and is) a major principle of the Commonwealth War Graves Commission that every man be commemorated on a headstone or have his name engraved on a Memorial to the Missing such as the Menin Gate. A search began to find the grave of Gordon Blackader. What had happened to the grave of this well-to-do Montrealer?

The first step was to get his Service Record. Unfortunately it gave no indication of what had happened to him. His next-of-kin was originally listed as his wife, Kathleen Blackader. Strangely her name had been crossed out and replaced by his little daughter, Patricia. This was a most unusual procedure. The mystery of Blackader remained unsolved until Jeffery Williams wrote "First in the Field", the biography of Hamilton Gault. Gault was the son of one of the wealthiest men in Canada. He had personally raised a battalion, the PPCLI, named after the Governor-General's daughter, Princess Patricia. As a Major he had been severely wounded and lost his leg on the same day his cousin, Gordon, was mortally wounded.

Williams wrote that the dying Blackader had asked Gault to take care of his wife and young daughter. Hamilton Gault, ever the respectable gentleman, agreed. Gault is one of the many interesting characters of the Canadian Expeditionary Force. Agar Adamson wrote with great admiration about this man, but he had his faults. One of them was always wanting his own way. He definitely had a bit of the spoiled child in him, but even that could never deter his sense of honour.

Although Gault remained in the Army he never returned to the front. He often lived in his Manor house in England and enjoyed touring the countryside in his auto. His relationship with Kathleen became stronger, and the recently-divorced (his divorce is also a very interesting story) Gault clearly admired the lovely widow. In November 1920 Hamilton Gault finally proposed marriage to the attractive Mrs. Blackader. All seemed well until November 1920, when driving through the English countryside Gault flipped his auto, Kathleen Blackader was severely injured and shortly after succumbed to her injuries. Gault then took her daughter Patricia as his ward for the next 13 years until Patricia began a relationship of which Gault disapproved. Consequently he decided to disown her.

From this story the change of Next-of-kin was understood, but where was Blackader buried? A chance call to Mount Royal Cemetery, Montreal in 1992 found out the location of the grave of Gordon H. Blackader. His family had brought his body home for burial, from England, like many well-to-do families did early in the war. Gordon Home Blackader was finally included in the records. The war affected many people beyond the killed and wounded. There were other types of casualties and no one kept records of them. Kathleen and Patricia Blackader will never be included in the records, although maybe they should be.

Gordon Home Blackader

Byng of the Byng's Boys

There are two milestones in the development of the Canadian Corps. The first was placing all Canadian Divisions in one, Nationally-based Army Corps. The second was the naming of Sir Julian Byng to command these divisions. Oddly both decisions were the results of petty Canadian politicking by Canada's energetic, erratic and very difficult Minister of Militia, Sam Hughes.

It was Sam Hughes' nationalism and ebullient character that ensured that all Canadian Divisions would serve together rather than be distributed throughout the British Army. It appears Lord Kitchener, the British Minister of War, would give Hughes virtually anything he wished rather than have to listen to him. It seemed to Kitchener that promotions and a knighthood certainly would not keep Hughes quiet but a Canadian Corps would (perhaps because Hughes envisioned himself as its commander).

The second milestone also involved Hughes' domineering character. This time it was another of his personality traits; the inability to admit he was wrong (like any politician). In this case the focal point was Hughes' pet project, the Ross rifle. Sir Sam had been instrumental in the development of the Ross, its manufacture in Canada, and its being the only rifle Canadian troops were allowed to use. This could have worked out well. The Ross was an excellent rifle under the right conditions. However the weapon required very tight tolerances on the diameter of the cartridges and the mass manufacturing methods of the day could not consistently produce cartridges to that tolerance. Consequently in action, using Lee-Enfield .303 ammunition, the rifle would often jam, with deadly consequences. The situation was so bad that Canadian soldiers often had to throw away their rifles and use discarded British Lee-Enfields.

The first General to command the Canadian Corps was a British regular army officer, Edwin Alderson. Alderson had commanded the Canadians at Ypres, Festubert and Givenchy in 1915 and St. Eloi Craters in 1916. His record throughout the fighting was undistinguished, but not bad. He had heard his men complaining about the Ross rifles, tested the weapon, surveyed the opinions of his officers, and concluded that the Ross must be withdrawn. Now, regardless of his record, Alderson was in direct opposition to Hughes and Hughes would not tolerate this. In a most blatant attempt to undermine Alderson's authority, Hughes sent a letter to all senior Canadian officers on how good the Ross rifle really was, and basically, what a fool Alderson was. Shortly afterwards, to avoid confrontation with Canada (Hughes) Kitchener replaced Alderson with Julian Byng.

Julian Hedworth George Byng was born in Wrotham, England on September 11th, 1862, the family's 13th child and seventh son. The young Julian showed little interest in school and "Bungo", as he was called, (his other brothers had the better names of Byngo and Bango), excelled in sport, and enjoyed playing the banjo. Coming from a long line of soldiers Julian Byng attested in the Militia at age 17 and at 21 became a Lieutenant in the 10th Hussars cavalry regiment and was posted to Lucknow, India. In 1884 the 10th Hussars sailed for England but were diverted to Egypt to participate in the war against the Mahdi and his Dervishes. In March 1884 Byng and the 10th Hussars took part in

Edwin Alderson

two successful attacks against the Mahdi at El Teb and later at Tamaai. After their two brief actions the 10th resumed its journey to England. It was Julian's first taste of war.

Over the next 15 years Byng gradually rose in the ranks. He proved himself to be more concerned with the welfare of his men than the pomp of Cavalry life. It was his charm and unorthodox character that would help him in his next adventure.

At the outbreak of the Boer War in 1899 the 37 year old Byng was sent to South Africa on the staff of General Redevers Buller. Buller made Byng a Lieutenant-Colonel in command of 600 irregular cavalrymen known as the South African Light Horse (SALH). Commanding such a band of colonials against such a determined and pragmatic foe as the Boer Commandos stretched Byng to his limit. In 1900-1901 Byng's SALH performed well even though the British Army suffered a number of stinging defeats This was a war unlike any others and required a line of thinking that was not taught at Staff College. It was dur-

Sir Sam Hughes

ing the Boer War that Byng was described as having "clear common sense", and that under fire he could be "absolutely depended upon". These would become his trademarks when he commanded the Canadians in 1916-1917.

At the end of the Boer War in 1902 Byng was shipped home and over the next 12 years he continued his rise up the ranks. At the outbreak of the First World War Julian Byng was given command of the 3rd Cavalry Division. They fought under his command at Zillebeke in October-November 1914 in the First Battle of Ypres and stayed in the Ypres Salient through the Second Battle of Ypres in April-May 1915. In August 1915 a major British Offensive at Gallipoli had met with stunning failure and Julian Byng was made a temporary Lieutenant-General, and given command of the 9th British Army Corps at Suvla Bay. He inherited a complete mess and after two months in command supported the evacuation of the peninsula. His views, although correct, put his former commander, Lord Kitchener, and his former subordinate, Winston Churchill, under severe criticism (and a Court of Enquiry) for the two had been the architects of the disastrous Gallipoli campaign. None-the-less the evacuation plan was approved and by early January 1916 all British troops were gone and Gallipoli was left to the Turks.

On February 1916 Sir Julian Byng returned to France and was given command of the 17th British Army Corps on the Vimy front.

In May 1916 Sir Julian Byng was 53 years old. He had been a soldier for 37 years, had handled Colonials successfully in the Boer War, had disagreed with Lord Kitchener, and had been bypassed when Herbert Gough, an officer, junior in service, was promoted over him and given command of a British Army. This led to him getting the Canadians.

Byng was well-suited to the men he was to command. He was not well-suited to handle the petty Canadian politicking of men like Sam Hughes. However he was a confident man, well-connected and not afraid of politicians. The timing of his arrival was also fortunate in that the Ross rifle confrontation (which had cost Alderson his job) was almost finished, as was the political career of Sam Hughes.

Within four days of taking command of the Canadians Byng was hit with his first catastrophe. On June 2nd 1916 the Germans blasted the Canadians off Mount Sorrel and threatened to collapse the Ypres Salient. To his credit Byng helped control an otherwise devastating situation and stemmed the German advance. Within 12 days he planned and executed a perfectly supported counter-attack that recaptured almost all of the lost ground. It was not quite a victory for the Canadians but snatched, at least some respectability, from the jaws of defeat.

The next major campaign for the Canadians was the Battle of the Somme in September-October 1916. Byng played a secondary role here as attacks were ordered by a higher command against uncut barbed-wire and without proper preparations and planning. The poorly planned attacks met with little success and heavy casualties. From these bloody attacks Byng learned important lessons. It was his old nemesis, Herbert Gough, who ordered the attacks.

At the end of October 1916 the Canadian Corps was moved to the Vimy front and it was here that Byng came into his own and the Corps became the Byng's Boys.

He set to work training his officers and men in special schools. He worked on discipline. He applied the lessons which he learned on the Somme: no attack would go forward without proper artillery preparation, objectives would be made clear and easy to identify, and German artillery would have to be taken out immediately after the attack started. In the winter of 1917 Byng set his whole plan in motion, the Canadians were to capture Vimy Ridge. But Byng's organizational skill was not his only ability that contributed to success. The men liked and trusted him. They were inspired by his presence, his confidence and his lack of pomp. He also cut through the petty jealousies that had hindered the Canadians in the early days.

When the day came, April 9th, 1917, Byng's Boys met all his expectations and in April and May 1917 when all British attacks in the Battles of the Scarpe failed it was only the Byng's Boys who succeeded.

In June 1917 Sir Julian Byng's successes were rewarded with promotion to full General and command of the Third British

Army. Even then he ensured the Canadian Corps would pass into competent hands. It was Julian Byng that promoted Arthur Currie, a Canadian, to command the Corps. Currie would follow Byng's blueprint and 1917 and 1918 would be years of great victories for the Canadians. (At Paschendaele Currie even refused to serve under Herbert Gough.)

Byng commanded the Third Army until the end of the war. He was the man behind the Battle of Cambrai in 1917, the first use of massed tanks in warfare. Although his Army was hammered in the German Offensives in March 1918, they stopped the Germans in front of Arras. (To the south the British Fifth Army was routed on the Somme and Herbert Gough, its Commander was duly sacked). Later in 1918 the Third Army participated in the Advance to Victory.

After the War Julian Byng prepared for a long-awaited retirement. This was not to be. In 1921 Sir Julian Byng was made the Governor-General of Canada, and he served happily and proudly in that capacity until 1926. In one of the saddest episodes in a long history of petty Canadian politics, Julian Byng, in many ways a founder of modern Canada, was ambushed by the ultimate petty politician, MacKenzie-King. MacKenzie-King's Liberals had been elected by a minority and could not form a Government. Byng, as the Governor-General, asked the Opposition to form the government and MacKenzie-King complained to England. Byng was recalled for meddling in Canadian politics. He was devastated by his recall, but perhaps he had been lucky. Petty politics took less than two years to get Alderson. It took 10 years to get to Byng.

Sir Julian Byng served as the Commissioner of Police at Scotland Yard from 1926-1932. He retired in 1932 and made one last visit to Canada. He travelled across Canada and every where he stopped he was met with great warmth and respect by the men he had led so magnificently in the war. After 16 years they were still Byng's Boys.

Julian Byng was the single most important reason the Canadian Corps became the force it was. And it was in no small way that those successes brought about the change in the hearts of his men. They went from colonials to proud members of the distinctly Canadian Corps. This change of heart, this pride transformed Canada into a nation.

It is sad that someone as important to our history as Julian Byng seems to be completely forgotten, as are the men he served with. The only modern legacy of Byng's is the trophy his wife donated in 1925 to be awarded to the Most Gentlemanly player in the National Hockey League. The Lady Byng trophy is still awarded annually.

Julian Byng died June 2nd, 1935.

Lieutenant-General Sir Julian Byng

FOR FURTHER REFERENCE

This guide has focussed solely on the actions of Canadian troops in the Battle of Mount Sorrel, 1916. However, fighting at Ypres was continuous throughout the war and hundreds of thousands were killed there. This included thousands of Canadians who died in the Second Battle of Ypres in 1915, at Passchendaele in 1917 and while holding the line from Ploegsteert to Hooge in 1915 and 1916. Being in the Salient was a curse for troops of all nationalities throughout the war.

Today, the Ypres Salient is the largest burial ground in the world. The monuments and cemeteries of the British, French, Belgians, Germans, Australians and New Zealanders are scattered throughout the salient. It is hard, even after all these years not to feel the overwhelming sorrow of the poor families who lost loved ones in this place. I have outlined below several books that will greatly increase understanding of the "Immortal Salient":

Before Endeavours Fade, by the late Rose Coombs (the best guide book on the Western Front), Battle of Britain Prints International, 1976.
Ypres, Then and Now, by J. Giles, Leo Cooper Ltd., 1970.
Ypres and the Battles for Ypres 1914-18, Michelin Guide, 1919.
Australian Battlefields of the Western Front 1916-18, by John Laffin, Kangaroo Press, 1992.
Thirteen Years After by W.R. Bird. CEF Books, 2000.

Books that pertain to the Battle of Mount Sorrel are almost nonexistent. Even after all these years only Lord Beaverbrook's "Canada in Flanders" covers the battle well. The books listed below are the best there are.

Canada in Flanders Volume II by Lord Beaverbrook. Hodder and Stoughton, 1917.
The Official History of the Canadian Expeditionary Force 1914-19, by G. W. L. Nicholson, The Queen's Printer, 1962.
Tapestry of War, by S. Gwynn, Harper Collins, 1992.
Byng of Vimy by J. Williams. Leo Cooper, 1983.
First in the Field by J. Williams. Vanwell Publishing, 1995.
The Journal of Private Fraser edited by R.H. Roy. CEF Books 1998
Letters of Agar Adamson edited by N.M. Christie. CEF Books 1997.

An amazing scene. Respect is shown for "The Fallen".
(Outside The Royal Exchange, London at The Eleventh Hour, 1927)